THE BUSINESS OF

THE BUSINESS OF

Seventeenth Edition, June 2013
(Formerly Published under the titles: *Leading
the Consumer Rebellion* and *Commerce Through
Community*)

Published by:

 Obstaclés Press
4072 Market Place Dr.
Flint, MI 48507

www.business-membership.com
www.business-membership.ca

Cover design and layout by Norm Williams, nwa-inc.com
Comic illustrations by Sean Catron

Printed in the United States of America

DEDICATION

We dedicate this book to those with the courage to pursue their dreams.

Go, therefore, and do
That which is within you to do;
Take no heed of gestures
Which would beckon you aside;
Ask of no man
Permission to perform.

"The Magic Story"
Frederick Van Rensselaer Day

CONTENTS

PREFACE TO THE
SIXTEENTH EDITION

Perhaps you are just starting out in life and are doing everything you've been taught in order to succeed. But every now and then you wonder if there might be a better way.

Perhaps you're fairly established. You have a decent job, a mortgage, a couple of car payments, and a little money put away for retirement. But every now and then, you wonder if there is something more out there.

Perhaps you've struggled financially for years, and no matter what you do it seems as if you can't get ahead. You save for a rainy day and then it floods. You can't help but wonder if there might be a better way.

Perhaps you have a heart for contribution and service to others. You give to charity, help out at church, take care of family members, and volunteer where needed. But you've wondered if you could make an even bigger impact.

Perhaps you've had a good career, raised a family, and have numerous accomplishments to your name. But you're not done. You know there is more you can do. Every so often you wonder if there is something bigger out there.

These scenarios represent the people we've met over the years, people who don't fall into a socio-economic group, classification, or demographic. They come from all walks of life, from all occupations and backgrounds, religions and cultures. But they do share four characteristics. These people are:

9

1. Ambitious
2. Looking for something more in life
3. Teachable
4. Honest

It is for such people we have written this little book. Our hope is that in the pages to follow you will find that something for which you've been looking.

Welcome to the LIFE you've always wanted.

1
BUSINESS OWNERSHIP

THE PURSUIT OF POSSIBILITIES

"I want to live while I'm alive," says the pop song. "Every man dies, not every man really lives," says William Wallace in the movie *Braveheart*. These phrases embody the spirit we have all felt at times. We want to live and experience the vast wonders of this world. We want to break out and run free.

Instead, many of us find our lives full of constraints with very little of what we might call living. Our career or occupation started with excitement but has somehow become a dull routine. Our incomes were once satisfactory but now get stretched paper-thin. Our vacation time seems shorter and fewer and farther between. When we look in the mirror, the old person we see startles us. We know time is passing, we know that we have dreams and aspirations that we haven't yet experienced, and we wonder if we will ever get around to them. It seems life is better at living us than we are at living it.

One of the best solutions to these dilemmas is the concept of personal business ownership. Being in business is seen by millions as the chance to take control of their financial futures and build something of lasting value. It is the door that opens to the pursuit of possibilities.

Ownership

The idea of ownership is not new, and has even found its way deep into the employee world. The concept of stock options was revolutionary in the business world and has become common throughout big business. Stock options provide enticement to executives to work for a "share" in the company, not just an income. Many times, in successful and growing companies, these stock options amount to much more than the executives' salaries. In progressive companies such as Blockbuster Entertainment Corp, leaders like Wayne Huizenga obtained massive commitments from employees through liberal use of stock options. Says author Gail DeGeorge, "Huizenga believed that to keep executives working for the benefit of shareholders, you had to make them think like shareholders. One difference, however, is that while many companies reserve options packages only for top executives, Huizenga believed in spreading stock incentives from the top throughout the executive ranks, and to employee ranks as well." Sam Walton of Wal-Mart had a similar philosophy. He said, "Plenty of companies offer some kind of profit sharing but share absolutely no sense of partnership with their employees. The more you share profits with your associates – whether it's in salaries or incentives or bonuses or stock discounts – the more profit will accrue to the company. Today, more than eighty percent of our associates own Wal-Mart stock." No doubt, this sense of ownership in these two highly successful companies, as well as thousands of others, has helped to inspire employees and spread a sense of ownership.

For many, this sharing in ownership of a large corporation is enough. But for countless others, there is a desire for something more.

Let's take a look at the typical corporate arrangement. An organizational chart or "org chart" is a diagram of boxes containing names of workers and showing their relationship in the corporation.

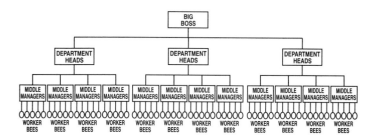

Generally, an org chart is shown whenever a new boss or manager arrives. One of their first objectives is to organize their staff and make sure everyone knows their position and lines of authority. Usually, the lowest "level" managers or workers are shown across the bottom, then the mid-levelers are shown next, and the bosses or department heads or CEOs are shown at the top. (Progressive companies will show an org chart tilted onto its side so nobody appears at the bottom.) In larger organizations like the automotive companies where we worked, the chain of command was so enormous that multiple org charts nested within each other! This allowed for many small ponds within the big pond.

Now, let us be clear. There is nothing wrong with the structure of corporations and businesses and the drawing out of org charts to explain them. In fact, our own administrative office is structured in just this way. The point is that to live within one of these charts is not acceptable to anyone who yearns for something more in their professional life. In the heart of millions of people beats the desire for one thing – ownership!

In the heart of millions of people beats the desire for one thing – ownership!

13

This need to own and create something of our own is natural. It is the very essence of the entrepreneurial spirit. It is what has driven folks like Henry Ford, George Eastman, Thomas Edison, Andrew Carnegie, Billy Durant, Mary Kay Ash, Bill Gates, and Michael Dell to develop the enormous companies we know today. Where would we be without the drive and creativity of these people and thousands like them? Where would we be if they had decided to get good, safe, secure jobs while ignoring the pangs of ambition they felt deep inside?

All of these people became very wealthy as a result of their efforts, though wealth was not the primary goal for any of them for long. Rather, wealth became a way of keeping score. According to Maury Klein, professor at the University of Rhode Island, "Money was for most of the great entrepreneurs a by-product of their real interest - important as both a personal reward and a way of keeping score - but not the driving passion behind their work." Even so, author Burke Hedges says it well: "So what is the secret of the wealthy anyway? I can answer that question in two words – they own. You see [they] understand that when you're an independent business owner, you're building your dream, not someone else's." Perhaps billionaire J. Paul Getty said it best in his book, *How To Be Rich*, written back in 1961, "Almost without exception, there is only one way to make a great deal of money in the business world – and that is in one's own business."

There it is: the desire to build one's own dream, to pursue one's own vision. At the heart of it that is what business ownership is about. Not the blatant pursuit of wealth, per se, but the chance for achievement uninhibited by corporate structures and layers of management that direct your efforts towards their goals instead of your own.

Bucket Carrying vs. Pipeline Building

In his landmark book, *The CASHFLOW Quadrant®*, Robert Kiyosaki introduces a concept of the same name, shown below.

In a very succinct way, Kiyosaki's diagram explains the four major ways to earn money in today's economy.

The "E" stands for employee; after college, that is where we made our start. This, in fact, is the biggest and most populated quadrant. Millions live each day and provide for their families as employees of someone else. The basic premise is that someone exchanges the doing of a task for an agreed upon amount of pay. This can happen in several ways: an hourly wage, a salaried wage or a commission. (These can also happen in combinations.) "Hourly pay" is the situation where an employer agrees to pay so much per hour for the task at hand; the way for the employee to make more money is to work more hours. Overtime work is a culture within itself, and many industries develop scores of people who grow accustomed to the increased hours and time-and-a-half pay. When times change, these people are left tightening their belts and selling their motorcycles. "Salary pay" is where an employer

15

agrees to an annual amount of compensation and then tries to cram as much work into the employees' year as possible. This is known throughout industry as "casual overtime." "Commission" is pay based only on performance.

In summary, though, the arrangement in the "E" quadrant is for an employee to trade hours for pay, plain and simple. College education or vocational training or journeyman status can elevate the amount of compensation, but the challenge in this quadrant is that eventually the worker is just simply out of hours to trade for pay. This arrangement eventually tops out. Sure there are raises throughout the years, but after a while the overall lifestyle is pretty consistent. Incidentally, it was the realization of exactly this point that drove us to look for a better way. We couldn't stand the thought of another 38 years to retirement at the same level of living we were already experiencing. We looked at people in our profession who were very good at their jobs, people who were 10 years further along than we were, and it became very obvious that to continue in the "E" quadrant would not produce any significant increase in lifestyle.

The "S" quadrant represents the "self-employed." We have always admired those who live in this column because generally some degree of risk and a serious level of competency accompany it. Self-employed people operate on their own, using their talents and training to earn income while reporting to nobody. In many ways, this lifestyle fulfills the urges of ownership we are discussing in this chapter. This category could include doctors, attorneys, accountants or any professionals in private practice. It could also include anybody who is an owner/operator of a business of his or her own. According to Kiyosaki, however, this quadrant ultimately boils down to the same arrangement as the "E" quadrant, the exchange of time for money. No matter what level of competency or professionalism on the part of the owner, his or her time is still required to make it a success. Again, what this leads to is a topping out of lifestyle, exactly where the owner runs out of personal time.

This leads us to the right side of the Quadrant. If the left side of the Quadrant was about trading time for money, either for an employer or for one's self, the right side of the Quadrant is about leverage. The concept of leverage, in fact, is the only true way to generate wealth. Leverage is the ability to multiply one's efforts in order to produce, over time, more return than the sum of the inputs. Without leverage, the most that can ever happen is an exchange of our efforts for dollars. After receiving the dollars, we must put in more effort to obtain more dollars.

Leverage is the ability to multiply one's efforts in order to produce, over time, more return than the sum of the inputs.

So what is there to leverage? First of all, we might think about our musical ability. Somebody actually wrote the song, *Happy Birthday* (believe it or not), and it produces large royalties on an annual basis. If we could just do something like that! In fact, no doubt, many readers of this book have musical ability. But the capability of writing music and having it gain widespread commercial acceptance is a very slender proposition. At least, it was not open to us! (Please don't ask us to prove it, not a pretty picture.) What about literary ability? Folks like John Grisham make millions off their books and movies. It works the same as music. Create something with commercial appeal and watch the royalties roll in. But again, while some of you reading this may be gifted in this area, this was not really available to us. What about inventions? It seems like everywhere we go people have great ideas kicking around in their heads that they want to patent and market. Great! Most of us don't have that option for any real, commercial gain. So then, if we

17

can't leverage our musical ability, our literary genius, or our inventiveness, then what is left for us average people to leverage? We don't want to spend our lives trading time for dollars on the left side of the Quadrant. As far as we know, there are only two viable options remaining.

The first of these is money. This is where the "I" quadrant comes in. "I" stands for "investor," and Kiyosaki calls it a "sophisticated investor" to differentiate from the majority of people out there who have a little money in their savings plans at work and own a mutual fund or two. For the purpose of his discussion, those people are not considered "investors" because they are not obtaining any significant leverage, at least not enough to live on. What Kiyosaki refers to is using large amounts of money to generate an ongoing income. The old saying goes, "What's the best way to make a small fortune? Start with a large one, preferably your spouse's father's!"

"B" business owners have a system to run their business so it can thrive and grow without their constant, daily inputs.

Seriously, large amounts of capital have the ability to generate ongoing, residual incomes. The problem for us, as with most people, is that we didn't have the large sum of money to begin with (and we married for love instead of money and had blown that chance, too!) So without large amounts of cash to invest to generate ongoing residual income structures, what were we left with?

We were left with the "B" quadrant, the "business owner." According to Kiyosaki, "B" business owners (as opposed to the "S" business owners) have a system to run their business so it can thrive and grow without their constant, daily inputs. What does that mean? What does a "B" business owner leverage? The only thing left, really. Not musical ability, not literary ability, not inventiveness, not even large sums of capital, but something everyone has in equal supply

– time. From the highest and the mightiest to the lowest of the low, we all get 24 hours a day, 168 hours a week. That's it - time - and what we do with it will make or break us.

We know what you might be thinking. Time!? Who's got time!? In fact, time is the one thing most people don't seem to have. We're so busy; we have to remind ourselves to go to the bathroom by typing it into our calendars!

We know. In fact, with our corporate careers and commutes to and from work and small families and household responsibilities and family obligatory duties, we were extremely time crunched. We had gotten to a point, where it seems many of us arrive, where we begin to think that being busy in and of itself is a sign of success. Henry David Thoreau said, "It is not enough to be busy, so too are the ants. The question is: what are we busy about?" Busy, busy, busy. "It must mean I'm important." Well, what we found, actually, was that it just meant we were busy. And we were getting old in a hurry and had very little time to take notice. So how in the world were we going to leverage time?

Our daily 24-hour pie chart looked something like this:

We discovered that we were wasting little bits of time on urgent but unimportant things that were literally robbing us of our productivity. And we were sacrificing enormous amounts of time to earn our paychecks that weren't ever going to take us higher in life. If we could squeeze out some discretionary time, maybe surrender some non-value added activities for a short while, we could have something worthy of leveraging: small doses of time on a consistent basis. That's exactly what we did.

The goal of leveraging time is a term we like to use called "regenerative income." A little illustration may be helpful (it was for us). Consider a situation in which a town has a need for a freshwater supply. For some reason, the supply runs out. The city council decides to put the supply of freshwater out for bids to willing suppliers. One is eventually chosen. That supplier begins delivering the water to the town by carrying buckets from the freshwater source to the town.

Applying the CASHFLOW Quadrant® to this example, we can see the "Es", or employees, showing up to work at the water source, picking up their assigned buckets and toting them repeatedly throughout the day to the town. Day after day, week after week, month after month, they show up to carry buckets. If they want to remain gainfully employed with the company and keep the paychecks flowing, they must continue to carry the buckets. Perhaps, as incentive, eventually they can earn some perks and benefits for being good bucket carriers, like having their title painted on the side of the bucket: "Senior Bucket Carrier," or maybe "Vice Executive Bucket Carrier Extraordinaire." Eventually, maybe they are provided a "company bucket" that they can park in their driveway so their neighbors can see how well they're doing at work. You get the idea.

The "S" business owner is the entrepreneur who received the contract for water delivery. It is her responsibility to provide buckets, supervise employees, make payroll, pay into Worker's Compensation and unemployment programs, make sure the water actually gets delivered, ensure the employees don't drink all of it, or spill it, or spit in it, etc. On really bad days, she may end up carrying buckets of water herself if she can't get enough of her crew to show up for work. Obviously some of this is fictional, but our "S" business owner friends assure us that these examples are not far off the mark. In fact, one "S" business owner commented that in his life the "S" stands for stress since everything eventually falls under his responsibility. "Some seasons it's feast, other seasons it's famine," he says. "You just never know."

The right side of the Quadrant works in a whole different way. Instead of the need to carry buckets at all, "Bs" (business owners) and "Is" (investors) utilize the concept of leverage or regenerative income. Rather than carrying buckets back and forth or ensuring that a group of employees does the work properly, the people on the right side of the Quadrant INVEST their time and/or money into constructing a pipeline. At first, the bucket carriers may actually appear to be ahead of the pipeline builders as water is carried to the town daily and pay is received. The pipeline builders may not even have all their permits yet and the "Es" and "Ss" on the left of the Quadrant are already making money. But it's similar to a 10-speed bicycle racing a jet airplane.

Don't trade your hours for dollars. INVEST your time and efforts into something that will bring long-term rewards.

The bike might dart out in front for an early lead, but once the jet gets momentum it's all over. Once the pipeline is finished and the water begins flowing to the town, the bucket carriers are most certainly out of business. The water is delivered automatically on an as-needed basis to the town; it is cleaner and more reliable, and the payments to the pipeline owners are made on a regular basis. Once the pipeline is built, most of the work is done, but the earning has just begun. That is regenerative income. Front-load the process with work (in real-life this usually turns out to be a lot of work) then eventually the money comes in cumulatively over time from those initial efforts. And even though any pipeline requires maintenance, it is minimal compared to the ongoing return.

That's truly what the right side of the Quadrant is all about: ongoing, regenerative income. Don't trade your hours for dollars. INVEST your time and efforts into something that will bring long-term rewards.

Accomplishing pipeline-type incomes wasn't easy for us, of course. And it didn't happen overnight. There were sacrifices along the way, but by carving out a little time on a consistent basis and leveraging it toward a "B" pipeline income; we were blessed with the ability to arrange our 24 hour pie chart exactly as we wanted.

As you can see, when done properly, a pipeline income allows flexibility. In fact, flexibility is one of the most desirable advantages of owning one's own "B" business. Many families would love to work fewer hours and spend more time together. Many young mothers would like the option of staying home during the years of their children's youth. Many people would love the time and the freedom to travel more, or to pursue hobbies and sports. How many fathers would love to attend their children's sports league events, perhaps even becoming a coach? It is this flexibility and freedom that makes the effort required to build a pipeline income worth it.

Tax Implications

There is another major advantage to owning one's own business: taxes, or more accurately, an improved plan for your tax burdens. For most people who earn their living by collecting a paycheck, as we did, the tax burden is enormous, because there are very few deductions available to someone who earns a living in the form of W-2 income. A W-2 statement goes from an employer to the United States government to report an employee's annual wages. The employee then has the option of declaring some allowable deductions, such as dependent children, mortgage interest, and charitable contributions (that is, if they have met the minimum requirement allowing them to itemize). But there is little else a W-2 recipient can do to reduce a tax burden. In fact, the better the "high paying job" pays, the worse the tax picture. In the business world, however, income is generated against a 1099 statement or a corporate tax return. The tax code encourages the growth of profitable businesses as an important part of economic growth for the country, therefore allowing deductions for legitimate expenses incurred in the pursuit of a profit. The earnings indicated on a 1099 or a corporate return are reduced by all allowable expense deductions. In many ways, this is a fairer arrangement than what is available to the W-2 recipient, and can possibly translate into more actual spending power.

We could go on for pages listing the reasons behind the enormous trend toward home-based businesses, "B" businesses in particular. People want freedom to pursue their own goals and dreams. They want to work and live as they please, where they choose. They want to earn as much as they are worth and not what the job or task is worth. They want to enjoy the best tax advantages available to maximize the results of their efforts; they want to live their lives instead of having their lives live them. They want ownership in something that matters and translates into real quality of life. As Maury Klein states, "Business lies at the heart of American culture and has long been the driving force in American history." More and more, people want to be a part of that force. In the next chapters we'll explain how that has become more possible than ever before.

2
FOUR INDUSTRIES

PERSONAL DEVELOPMENT, HOME-BASED BUSINESSES,
LIFE COACHING, AND COMMUNITY BUILDING

Opportunity can be defined as, "A favorable combination of circumstances." In the business world this usually involves the exploitation of trends favorable to the endeavor. As the saying goes, "An idiot in a straight-up trend defeats an expert in a flat one every time!" While we are not claiming to be experts, we do know a great trend when we see one.

Further, it has been said that success occurs when opportunity and preparedness meet. If that is true, then it should be even more so at the intersection of four explosive trends or industries!

Industry #1: Personal Development

"Excuse me, can you direct me to the self-help section?" we asked the bookstore employee.

"Well, if I told you, it would defeat the purpose, wouldn't it?"

All kidding aside, there is no ignoring the immensity of the industry loosely known as Personal Development. This broad category may also rightly be called the Leadership or Leadership Development industry, the Self-Help industry, or the Training industry. Perhaps the broad range of names for this

25

category demonstrates just how large this sector of the economy has become.

From official corporate training to an individual reading a people skills book, and everything in between, the Personal Development industry has become a force to be reckoned with. Most estimates put its overall annual revenue in the neighborhood of $400 billion.

The origins of Personal Development go back as far as Aristotle and Confucius. Personal Development has found footing in business, major universities, research institutions, and in the lives of ambitious individuals. In short, it has become almost a universally accepted truth that improvement follows personal growth. More skills, more understanding, better perspective, clearer insight, and adherence to time-tested principles have proven to be critical for career, professional, personal, financial, and relational advancement. For this reason, personal development books, materials, conventions, conferences, and mentoring are now available in nearly every category of endeavor.

A quick look at the marketplace will reveal that if you are not taking advantage of the wealth of material available for self-improvement and advancement, you are missing the proverbial boat.

Industry #2: Home-Based Businesses

The original appeal of the concept of networking, or what was once called network marketing, remains as strong today as it was at its birth. That appeal speaks to the very things we discussed in chapter one: the chance for business ownership.

There is something very right about an opportunity to own one's own business. There is something very right about compensation that flows to the performer and isn't subject to boardroom politics, gender, age, race, religion, or any other prejudices. There is something very right about a business flexible enough to allow one to go as fast or as slow as is possible or desired. And there is something very right about a business that is affordable to begin, sustain, and grow over time. Finally, there is something very right about an opportunity that is only limited by one's ability, and not by anyone else's assessment of that ability.

For all these reasons and more, networking has expanded around the world, prospering in nearly every region and within nearly every culture. Experts estimate the annual global revenue of the networking industry to be around $100 billion. People married and single, young and old, prosperous or financially strapped, and from nearly every other extreme have succeeded mightily in this industry.

Networking is unique in that it generally requires very low start-up costs and relies more upon one's personal initiative and persistence than capital and equipment. Networking runs on the power of people to leverage one of the most potent marketing approaches ever discovered: word of mouth. In short, friends do what friends do, and connecting relationships together with a chance to Have Fun, Make Money, and Make a Difference (the Team's motto) is rewarding on many levels.

Industry #3: Life Coaching

The Life Coaching industry is relatively new, but still, in a short amount of time it is already estimated to be over $1.5 billion annually. Wikipedia explains it as, "the practice of supporting an individual, referred to as a choachee or client, through the process of achieving a specific personal or professional result." Well, that sounds pretty boring. If that were all it consisted of, we're sure it wouldn't be the growing market that it is.

Rather, what makes the Life Coaching industry so hot is the fact that people are waking up to the possibility that they have blind spots in their thinking. Coaches can provide a window into these blind spots. As the saying goes, "You don't look like what you look like when you look at yourself." Coaches stand apart and outside of you and therefore can offer you a perspective different from, and often times, more accurate than your own. From such a vantage point, coaches offer perspective and protection against self-deception. And who isn't at least a little bit self-deceived? Anyone who would say they weren't at least a little self-deceived would be, well, self-deceived.

Of course, the best coaches are those who have proven success, who have the so-called "fruit on the tree," and "walk the talk." They have experience, wisdom, and results. They are able to provide the best assistance to the development of someone else's thinking precisely because they have undergone the successful transformation of their own. In other words, great coaches are necessary to help you think through whether you should think what you think you should think.

Industry #4: Community Building

Okay, this one really isn't an industry at all, but something much bigger. It encompasses the entirety of the human need for connection to others. We are built to be relational creatures: in relationship with our family, friends, neighbors, and Creator.

Sadly, this desired state of harmonious relationship is often lacking. Institutions that once thrived in this area have faltered in our busy high-stress society. Church leaders have complained of people's apathy and lack of involvement. Clubs and organizations have seen their numbers dwindle. Commutes to work and crammed schedules have separated us from small moments of intimacy with neighbors and friends. Spontaneity and casual conversations are almost extinct, lost in the blur of time-management and minute-by-minute parceling out of our days. Into this void of meaningful connections has rushed a relatively new concept that has quickly become a phenomenon. Almost no one, including its pioneers, saw it coming. This new concept is called Social Networking. It consists of electronic communication in small doses and the false sense of "friendship" through shared space on a website. Although there are certainly many positives that can be gained through an Internet connection to others, such as staying in touch with long-lost college roommates, extended family, old friends and former neighbors, and meeting people of shared interests, the down-side is that many have come to replace "the real thing" with false, shallow, Online relationships. We can "friend" and "unfriend" someone with the click of a button. We can attract "followers" who may not even be listening. We can fool ourselves that we've got relationships when all we have are pale shadows of acquaintances.

Through it all, however, the deep-seated human need for true connection remains. It will not go away. For this reason, there exists a huge potential wherever and whenever someone can provide a truly meaningful community environment in a way that combines both the high tech and the high touch aspects of today's society. The best combination is a community-based organization that comprehends today's busy, high-tech world but still manages to bring people together in real and meaningful ways. That's true community building, and there's more of a need for it today than ever.

Opportunity

Author Frans Johansson in *The Medici Effect* wrote about the difference between *directional innovation* and *intersectional innovation*. He defines directional information as incremental improvement in a product or service. This might be considered baby-step innovation, or continuous improvement. Intersectional innovation, however, is revolutionary; it results in the combining of things never before combined. Intersectional innovation generally results in something explosive, something new, and something exponentially better than anything that existed before. As Howard Berke, cofounder and chairman of Konarka said, "If you identify the confluence between two industries it can form the basis for a new industry. Each company I started has been at the intersection of at least two industries. It is a deliberate strategy; it is how you innovate." As Johansson wrote, "The secret is this: If you want to create something revolutionary, head toward the intersection."

Consider this: if such explosive innovation is available at the intersection of two industries, imagine what could happen at the intersection of *four*? In short, that's the LIFE business: the intersection of the four industries of Personal Development, Home-Based Businesses, Life Coaching, and Community Building.

LIFE is the explosive business that takes the best of each of these four categories and combines them into something revolutionary.

3
PERSONAL DEVELOPMENT

YOU DON'T KNOW WHAT YOU DON'T KNOW

It has been said the best investment you can make is in yourself. Truly, your only real security is your own ability to perform. Getting better, improving yourself, gaining skills, growing in your thinking, staying sharp, and broadening your horizons are critical in a world that is changing more and faster than ever. But just how is one to do all this?

For many, the answer to that question has been found in the Personal Development industry. In order to advance their own abilities and understanding, millions and millions of people have tapped into the expertise and information provided therein. After all, we *are* in the Information Age. Information is now so prevalent the trouble is no longer in getting access to information but rather in gleaning out the *right* information. And what exactly comprises the *right* information? Simple: information from the correct source – meaning, information from those who have already demonstrated and/or experienced success.

The great shortcut to personal greatness is not in trial and error, which is time consuming and frustrating (with the additional benefit of sometimes being embarrassing), but rather in following the example of others who have more experience. In short, the best experience is someone *else's*.

Therefore, what information is the most important? That which brings the biggest benefit to the recipient. It is this upon which the entire Personal Development industry has been built.

You Don't Know What You Don't Know

There is a cute saying that states: "You don't know what you don't know." And really, how *could* we? But there's more. Not only do we not know what we don't know, but also we are forgetting much of what we used to know. When we consider our formal training as engineers, for instance, it is embarrassing how much of it we've lost. But this cute little jingle goes even further. Not only do we not know what we don't know, and we are forgetting much of what we did know, but also some of what we know just isn't so. Think about it. How many things have you learned that turned out not to be true? It happens all the time. Take song lyrics, for example. Have you ever been caught singing along with a song on the radio and someone pointed out your (likely hilariously) incorrect understanding of the actual words? So any one of us has such a small lock on knowledge that it makes sense to be constantly learning.

An Improved LIFE

The purpose of the LIFE business is to provide a better life for its customers. As we like to say, "Our finished product is a better life." This is accomplished through world-class information in the form of audio recordings (CDs and downloads), videos (DVDs and video clips Online), books, pamphlets, packs, events, and other resources. The format or media utilized are incidental – it's the information itself that has the power to transform lives.

The 8 Fs

There are eight channels through which LIFE materials seek to have a positive impact. These are listed here alphabetically:

1. Faith
2. Family
3. Finances
4. Fitness
5. Following
6. Freedom
7. Friends
8. Fun

These comprise the spokes of a wheel, representing the broad categories through which we live our lives. Interconnected and in balance, our wheel steers the ship of our lives. Out of balance and fractured, we are lost in the wind and tossed about on the seas. Only by grabbing firmly the spoke most needed at the moment can one gain control over one's life and steer toward calmer seas.

The power of this arrangement of information is in its broad applicability. We have never met the person who didn't need help in at least one of these categories. There is probably even an argument to be made that all of us could and should be working to improve in each of these categories all the time.

Still, we must prioritize. An interesting exercise would be to rank these 8 F's in the order most important to you right now. In which of these areas could you stand to learn and grow? Which of these areas is causing you the most heartache and pain right now? These are the types of considerations LIFE customers make as they grab the correct spoke and choose materials to help them improve their lives.

Credibility

Of course, information is only valuable if it works. And, quite frankly, there is a lot available in the broader Personal Development industry that may be considered questionable. Who hasn't chuckled at late night "infomercials" promising wealth and happiness through strange mind-control techniques or mystical hogwash? So how do you know good information from the rest? Again, it goes back to whether the information has been demonstrated to effectively transform lives, and this is often a difficult thing to quantify.

The first place one might look is to satisfied customers. The *Launching a Leadership Revolution* book, for instance, is a NY Times, Wall Street Journal, Business Weekly, Money Magazine and USA Today bestseller. In all, our books have sold nearly 1 million copies. Critics such as Publisher's Weekly, Alltop Leadership Selection, Leadership Guru lists, online masters degrees, college textbooks, Online corporate video training, and private business consultants have either provided positive press, recommendations, or have utilized our materials in their own work.

34

All that is certainly well and good, and we are appreciative and humbled by this response to what we do. However, there is nothing like the power of personal testimony from our customers to reassure us that our best efforts have not been in vain. When someone's life has truly been changed for the better, there is the added benefit that they usually can't shut up about it. Conveniently, we've provided a channel where customers of the LIFE products can contribute their stories. These can be accessed on the LIFE website, www.the-life-business.com. Behind the Testimony button is a plethora of customer commentary and video snippets depicting their experience with both the LIFE information and the business itself, complete with a search engine where one can compare results across occupations, financial standing, marital status, etc.

Value

Value can be defined as worth over cost. Perhaps nowhere does a greater variability of value exist than in the Personal Development industry. In fact, it is in this area where much of the knocks against the industry occur.

A brief review of industry prices will quickly demonstrate why. Below are some prices on actual materials and events taken at random from websites of many of the industry's top names:

1. A three day workshop and seminar focused on personal mastery – price $1997
2. 6 CDs and 1 DVD comprising a home study course in success – price $395
3. A 14 DVD set on effective management – price $789
4. A success strategy blueprint consisting of 6 DVDs and 1 CD – price $299

5. A series on how to master money which includes receiving 2 CDs per month – price $67 per month
6. A three day conference teaching great leaders how to lead teams – price $1895

Don't get us wrong. We have learned from and enjoyed materials from each of these providers (who shall remain anonymous). There is nothing wrong with the information they provide, nor the prices they are able to command in the marketplace. In fact, more power to them!

However, such prices put these materials out of the reach of most people, thereby relegating them to the upper echelon of our society in terms of financial ability. It is our firm belief, though, that this type of information is not only valuable but also needed by a broader market of people. After all, when we first started out in business we were both deep in debt and had only minimal (and sometimes no) resources to invest. Therefore, the pricing strategy of LIFE materials is perhaps the most aggressive in the industry. For instance, audio recordings are generally just $10 when purchased individually, and even less when purchased in combination with others in subscriptions. DVDs, books, pamphlets, and events are similarly low, with an overall average of being 70 to 300% cheaper than the competition.

Compensation

There is another enormous point to be made here, though, even at risk of getting ahead of ourselves in the flow of this book. Consider if you will, all the money that is made on the materials in the Personal Development industry. Who gets that money? The answer is the creators of the material and their companies that produce them. That's it. This is one reason some are so fabulously wealthy and can show such high lifestyles on their infomercials.

In the case of the LIFE business, however, that money is put back into a compensation plan through which any LIFE member can earn and prosper. Not only are LIFE materials extremely low priced, but the profits are shared with LIFE business participants based upon performance according to a pay plan (see the Income Disclosure Statement available on the LIFE website). Talk about value!

The Brasini Theory

We often don't know we are a crooked line until someone shows us a straight one. That is the net effect of providing information that is tied to timeless truths. It has the power to transform lives by demonstrating what is possible through a clear example.

In her bestseller *That Summer in Sicily,* author Marlena De Blasi tells the story of a nine-year old girl sold by her merchant father to a rich prince. The father is cold-hearted and cruel, and repeatedly spurns the little girl's love and attempted returns to her familial home.

Once the little girl grows up and becomes a woman of her own in the prince's home, she inquires of him about her situation. The prince assures her he had nothing but the best intentions for her, but returns to her a question of his own. He asks her how she managed to emerge from such hurtful abandonment by her father without herself growing bitter. She answered by relating an experience she had in the village market one morning.

"I never forgot that," she replied, "the way Signor Brasini just stopped and turned to his wife, put his big farmer's hands out and caressed her face, pulled her close to him and kissed her just like in the films. He kissed her for a long time and then looked at her and smiled . . . And when I saw all that, I knew that their way would be my way. Their way, not my father's . . . way – their way was how I wanted my life to be. I knew that someday I would be loved by a man like Brasini. *I understood how things worked and how they didn't work.*"

The young girl had gotten better information. Her whole life up to that point had been cold and full of bitterness. She had been mistreated and neglected. Yet as soon as she saw an example of what *could* be, in fact what *should* be, she was forever transformed. She had seen how things worked and how they didn't work.

That's the power of information from the correct source, of information from those like Signore Brasini. And that, dear reader, is what the LIFE materials are designed to do – provide a warm kiss in the village market for all the world to see – a straight line for all those who've never seen anything but a crooked one. Be it in finances, relationships, spiritual matters, or any of the other 8 Fs, we know that providing a rock-solid example is the most important kind of information. It is a pressing issue for us, in fact, a passion. We are as passionate about spreading truth into the lives of people in order to help them as old Brasini was about his peasant wife. And we'll be laying out straight lines in the marketplace as long as anyone is watching.

4

NETWORKING

UTILIZING THE PRINCIPLES OF FRANCHISING AND THE
POWER OF WORD-OF-MOUTH MARKETING

Watching what actually runs and controls a business best indicates whether the enterprise is an "S" business or a "B" business. "S" business owners are in control of their businesses themselves, but a "B" business is not run by the owner, but by a "system." An "S" business owner must be there to keep things running smoothly. A "B" business owner has a system that runs things smoothly. Michael E. Gerber in the book *The E Myth* states, "The system runs the business. The people run the system. The question you need to keep asking yourself is: How can I give my customer the results he wants systematically rather than personally? Put another way: How can I create a business whose results are systems-dependent rather than people-dependent?"

Franchising is one answer to this question. The word franchise originally came from the French, meaning to be "free from servitude." A franchise business is one in which somebody has already developed a successful system of operation and offers the use of that system for sale to prospective business owners. The new business owners, called franchisees, pay a fee to purchase the rights to the operating system from the franchiser and agree to follow corporate rules and regulations. Gerber says the franchiser "not only lends its name to the smaller enterprise, but it also provides the franchisee with an entire system of doing business." There are two enormous benefits to a franchise business arrangement:

1. Expertise and experience provided in systematic form
2. Exponential business growth through the power of duplication

Expertise and Experience

A commonly heard phrase states: "Experience is the best teacher." This, however, is only a partial truth. While we can all agree that much learning is accomplished through first-hand experience, it is not true that it is the best teacher. Personal trial and error, while educational, can be time intensive and sometimes painful, too. The *best* teacher is actually somebody else's experience. A rare shortcut in business is to learn from the mistakes of others.

One of the key principles of franchising is that a wealth of business experience, in the form of specific, practical knowledge, is made available to the franchisee. This saves a lot of time and anguish, and is designed to provide success for the independent franchisee. This knowledge and experience is given in the form of an operating system. The operating system is a set of procedures and business practices that have proven successful. The franchisee merely has to apply his or her efforts and energy and the operating system does the rest.

> *One of the key principles of franchising is that a wealth of business experience, in the form of specific, practical knowledge, is made available to the franchisee.*

Of course, there are companies that are better than others at franchising their experience and growing a successful business. But the principle is a sharing of expertise so that both parties can win. If the independent franchisees thrive, the parent company benefits as well. If franchisees fail, the parent company loses too. This is the classic business case of the "win-win" philosophy. As with the history of Ray Kroc and McDonald's, it has proven to be a revolutionary business trend, permeating nearly every facet of our society. Franchising has been effective for products and industries as varied as fast food and pet grooming or video rentals and overnight shipping.

In order to see just how revolutionary this concept was when it began to catch fire in the 1960s, let's go back to the way businesses have historically operated. It used to be, and still is in many industries, that business experience and trade secrets are the very lifeblood of a business. Business is a dog-eat-dog world, and everybody is wearing dog-biscuit underwear! For someone to actually make it in the business world was, and is, quite an accomplishment. The experience gained along the way becomes almost priceless. To share these "trade secrets" with anyone outside the company would be a mistake. Don't train your apprentices too well, or they may be your newest competitors when you bid on the next job. But franchising changed all of that. Gerber says, "Where eighty percent of all businesses fail in the first five years, seventy-five percent of all business

It has been said, "The best way to walk through a minefield is to follow in the footsteps of someone who has successfully crossed."

format franchises succeed!" Indeed, franchising has made the sharing of business operating secrets, or "mentoring," a profitable exchange for both parties. It has been said, "The best way to walk through a minefield is to follow in the footsteps of someone who has successfully crossed."

Picture an inexperienced, ambitious person wanting to go into business. If success is like crossing a minefield, the rookie stands at the edge and attempts to cross. That is conventional business. But franchising provides the new recruit with a map and a guide. The minefield is navigable because someone demonstrates the way through. All the franchiser needs is an ambitious participant willing to listen. All the franchisee needs is someone to show the way.

From time to time, we are confronted by someone asking, "What are you really selling?" A trite answer to that question is, "We are selling a map through the minefield." Without such a map, there are only a couple choices. First, never even try. Leave the minefield to others and stay where you are in life. Second, venture in on your own and take your chances (you might want to plug your ears).

Exponential Growth Through Duplication

By developing an operating system that truly works, a business can expand rapidly by finding entrepreneurs to establish franchise locations throughout a given area. If the system is effective enough, the growth can be exponential. This is because of a concept called *duplication.*

Let's use McDonald's again as an illustration. As the pioneers in large scale franchising, the company definitely has a system. When you go into your local McDonald's, where is the counter? Where is the fry machine? Where is the drive-up window? What color are the arches? What is on the menu? We predict that most of these answers concerning your local Mc-Donald's are nearly the same as ours. Further, think about the average employees you see in a McDonald's restaurant. Who are they? Are they industry experts, experienced in multiple areas of food service? Are they veterans of fast food retailing? Certainly some are, particularly the managers; but the vast major-ity of the employees are minimum wage employees, just starting out in life and probably working their first job. Here is one of the most consistently success-ful food companies in the world, and it does it with a mostly entry-level workforce. How does McDonald's do it? The company has a highly tuned operating sys-tem, right down to the last detail. It's the same every-where you go.

This didn't happen by accident. According to Mi-chael Gerber, "Ray Kroc began to look at his business [McDonald's] as the product, and at the franchisee as his first, last, and most important customer. Forced to create a business that worked in order to sell it [to franchisees], he also created a business that would work once it was sold, no matter who bought it. Armed with that realization, he set about the task of creating a foolproof, predictable business. A systems-depen-dent business, not a people-dependent business." It is the results of these efforts that produced a business that can be run profitably by anyone, even entry level, minimum wage employees.

How did Kroc do it? Unlike other attempts at fran-chising, his system left the franchisee with as little operating discretion as possible. Discretion is the enemy of duplication. The more things can be standardized, the more automatic success will be for each franchise. The more things left to chance or interpretation, the less the idea will duplicate. Gerber says, "If you're doing everything differently each time you do it, if everyone in your company is doing it by their own discretion, their own choice, rather than creating order, you're creating chaos." Ultimately, what Kroc developed was a system that kept things simple, kept them the same, and provided an enormous business opportunity to potential franchise owners. And his system duplicated like wildfire and led to exponential business growth.

> *Discretion is the enemy of duplication. The more things could be standardized, the more automatic success would be for each franchise.*

The Team System

Franchising isn't for everyone. When we started in the business world, we couldn't even afford a ticket to the franchise game. While all these concepts of learning from somebody with experience, following their map through the minefield and learning to duplicate proven operating techniques sounded exciting, we still didn't have any money; franchises have become extremely expensive over the years since Kroc's pioneering days, and they may or may not be the opportunity they once were. The principles, however, remain. That is why we have taken so much time dissecting what Kroc did at McDonald's.

What we found was a way to tap into years of business experience from like-minded people who had succeeded in endeavors similar to what we were attempting. We started reading and asking and listening. We realized that we didn't know what we didn't know, and that the thing we were most ignorant about was what we were ignorant about. Our biggest blind spot was the blind spot we didn't know we had, but we could tap into the success of others, who in turn would benefit from our success. It was a great way to experience the principles of franchising without the high ticket to entry, not to mention the stipulations and liabilities. Most importantly, it worked.

From this concept, the Team training system was born. To help people build communities of people who merchandise LIFE products, we have a map through the minefield. This map, or our system, satisfies the two big precepts of franchising: the sharing of experience and the power of duplication.

The Team system is audio training (compact discs and downloads), visual training (books and videos), association with people who have succeeded (meetings), and most importantly - mentors. This system provides training and education in two major categories: timely material and timeless principles. Timely material involves techniques and methods. These change with the times and the business climate. Timeless principles are true today and will be true tomorrow. They always work and provide a foundation for success. The saying is: "Methods are many; principles are few. Methods always change; principles never do."

This system provides training and education in two major categories: timely material and timeless principles.

Since ninety-five percent of people make money as employees ("E's") or through self-employment ("S's"), one of our system's biggest objectives is to help people develop from ninety-five percent thinking (or the left side of the CASHFLOW Quadrant®) to five percent and above thinking (the right side of the Quadrant). This is because changes in our results in life must follow changes in our thinking. The equation looks like this:

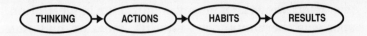

Change your thinking, and action will follow. Consistently change your actions, and you'll create new habits. A change in habits leads to changed results. In essence, to change your results in life (output), you need to change your thinking (input).

John Maxwell says, "The problem with most educational institutions is that they try to teach people what to think, not how to think. People must learn how to think well to achieve their dreams and to reach their potential." Said John Jacob Astor, "Wealth is largely a result of habit." One of the most poignant statements concerning the importance of thinking comes from Ravi Zacharias, who said, "I now wonder what blessings I have robbed myself of in life for not pausing to think." Success measures each of us to the exact dimensions of our thinking.

Word-of-Mouth Marketing and the Power of Relationships

The networking industry utilizes more than just the principles of franchising, however. Also at work is the amazing power of word-of-mouth marketing. This is the cheapest and most effective form of advertising. Personal relationships are still one of the most powerful forces in the business world, and the networking industry provides a way for people to leverage their network of contacts and acquaintances into a growing business that soon spreads beyond those they know.

In fact, this is one of the most peculiar aspects of the concept of networking. A person's success doesn't really hinge upon the size or quality of his or her already established network of friends and associates, but rather quickly grows beyond that. What really counts is a person's ability to build bonds with people over time while working on business objectives together. Serving others, helping them to plug into the training system, and aiding them in the success of their businesses, all play a bigger role in the spreading of markets from person to person. It's a business that builds relationships as it goes, developing bonds of personal trust through shared experiences and success, not merely building upon already existing relationships.

In fact, often times one's biggest business partners are people one didn't even know when beginning the business. In this way, networking is actually a business transcendent of word of mouth marketing. More accurately stated, it is a power of relationship business. People are the purpose, not the means. As the Team likes to say, "This isn't a business we build with purpose; this is a purpose we build with a business." That purpose is helping people through helping people help people.

5
LIFE COACHING

YOU DON'T LOOK LIKE WHAT YOU LOOK LIKE
WHEN YOU LOOK AT YOURSELF

The crowd is in a frenzy and the stands are shaking under the weight of fifty thousand people jumping and cheering. It's a crisp fall day but the sky is clear and blue. A gust of wind upsets the hair of the only person not moving at all – the coach. He stands there rigid and motionless in the center of the maelstrom, holding a clipboard and staring intently out at the field. Thinking. Deciding. Then, finally, he's made his choice.

"Go for it!" he says to his assistant coach, and the offense rushes out onto the field. The fans go wild.

This is likely the image we have of a coach - someone who is in charge of making the decisions, the tough calls, of standing tall when the pressure is intense, of dealing with the press and the players and the opposition. But there is much more to the job of coaching than the "captain of the ship" position demonstrated on game day. In fact, that really isn't the biggest part of coaching at all.

The term coach can be defined as, "something that takes you from where you are to where you want to go." Obviously, that is a different meaning for the word "coach." It is reminiscent of Cinderella's transportation to the ball. But isn't it interesting that this definition works for a human coach as well? For, in fact, a coach is someone who helps you get where you'd

49

like to go. An effective coach understands how to get you to do what you already want to do. An effective coach can see you, not only for what you already are, but also for what you can eventually become. In fact, it is this ability to "see" that enables coaches to help their protégés.

Knowing How to See

Leonardo da Vinci (1452-1519) of the High Renaissance period was an avid sketcher and note taker. This was his technique of fulfilling what he called *saper vedere*, "knowing how to see." It was, he claimed, the secret to his art.

This 'knowing how to see" is exactly what a coach provides. With an outside perspective, and hopefully with superior knowledge and experience, a coach can provide a window for "seeing better." This is critical because improvement can only be built upon a foundation of facts. An honest assessment must be made. The best coaches can see clearly where someone is, and then make informed recommendations for change and improvements.

It is upon this principle that the Life Coaching industry was built. People of all walks and occupations have recently taken to hiring coaches to help them "up their game." Coaching, it seems, isn't just for athletes anymore, and rightly so.

Fruit on the Tree

There is a challenge, though, with all this new-found respect for coaching, and that challenge is competence. Although coaches aren't always more successful than their protégés, they must be able to demonstrate a track record of helping others improve. Most of the time this means the coach is further down the road than the protégé. As we said earlier, the best experience is someone else's, and preferably, someone who already has "fruit on the tree."

This is why we emphasized credibility in Chapter 3. For someone to submit himself or herself to the coaching process in order to improve, he or she must be able to wholeheartedly rely upon the information being provided. This is where the LIFE business shines, as proven material is readily at hand in each of the 8 F categories to help people improve. And, through the Team training system and the community of other LIFE members, coaching and mentoring is available from those with fruit on the tree.

The Price of Resisting Change

It has been said the only people who like change are babies. This is because change can often be uncomfortable. We like things how they are, at least compared to the unknown. But change for improvement sake is one of the healthiest and most productive things we can do.

The tendency to resist change and remain blind to one's shortcomings has many parallels in history. In 1346, England's King Edward III and his army of about 8,000 soldiers became completely surrounded by a significantly larger French army in an area called Crecy. Estimates of the size of the French assault run from a count of 12,000 to over 100,000 knights and soldiers. According to author Richard Luecke, "The English were far from home, outnumbered, and without lines of support." But, unbeknownst to their French attackers, the English had a superior system, and it was known as archery.

The Welsh bowmen had become the best archers in the world, and their culture had lifted it to an art form that would change the course of medieval warfare in one fateful day. Writes Luecke, "Good archers could hit a human target at 100 meters; they could hit a formation target at 300 meters; and they could nock and deliver between ten to fifteen arrows per minute. It is said that an English arrow could penetrate two to three inches of oak, which meant that is was capable of piercing chain mail and, if struck directly, some of the armor plate worn by knights and men-at-arms." The French, certainly, had their archers, too. These were crossbowmen known as Genoese. Their method and technology dated back to the 12th century. A skilled crossbowman could get off two good shots in a minute. Says Luecke about the battle that day at Crecy, "Upon a signal from the French commander, the Genoese cranked up their crossbows and let their bolts fly at the English, but this first volley fell short. Before they could reload and advance into range, the English archers unleashed a barrage that must have appeared like a dark swarm of hornets lofting into the sky, hanging there briefly before raining down with a thousand hissing voices. Another volley followed within seconds – and another, and another. The Genoese tumbled by the hundreds. Without armor or shelter they were totally defenseless against the murderous rain of English arrows. The few unscathed among them fled in terror . . ." Next came the French horsemen, the gallant knights in their shining armor. The arrows cut them like a scythe. Once off their horses, they were easy prey for English footmen with axes.

Incredibly, the French sent fifteen separate assaults like this directly against the English line, each ending in disaster. The final battle tally: 16,000 dead French, about 300 Englishmen lost. The story, however, continues. The two sides met again ten years later at the Battle of Poitier. The result was the same as before, with the French forces left in total decimation. Then unbelievably, fifty-nine years later it happened again! The French attackers outnumbered the English army four-to-one, but the same lopsided victory resulted. English King Henry V lost less than 150 men to an estimated 6,000 French dead.

Most interesting about this incredible string of massacres is the managerial reason behind it. Luecke says, "England's tactical combination of archers with men-at-arms was an innovation that successfully challenged the military technology of the time. . . How did the French respond? The evidence indicates that they did not adopt massed archery in the reform of their own forces. To do so would be to give ground to the idea that a peasant in a leather helmet with a bunch of slender arrows in his belt was in some way a match for his social superior [the armored knight]. Instead of adopting the new military technology for themselves, the French merely invested more deeply in what they already had, and what had worked so well for them in the past."

We appreciate this bit of history because it shows exactly what can happen when old ideas resist the new. If taken to the extreme, it results in massacre. John Maynard Keynes said, "The difficulty lies not so much in developing new ideas, as in escaping from the old ones."

That is the job of good coaching. Those who refuse to grow and get better will likely be hearing arrows in the sky. In other words, the lesson is repeated until the lesson is learned.

6
BUILDING COMMUNITIES
THE THREE CS AND THE CONCEPT OF CONNECTEDNESS

Before the Team's approach to building communities was even on the drawing board, our desire to be involved in a business of our own led us to start independent relational marketing businesses. We struggled for a few years but gained valuable experience. Then in 1999 two major events changed everything. First, we experimented with some strategies that really started to work. Second, through a web-based merchandizing concept, our base of operations became the Internet. We next got the opportunity to attend a luncheon at which billionaire founder of Dell Computer Corporation, Michael Dell, was the keynote speaker.

There were many reasons we were excited to attend the event. First, Michael Dell is a hero to almost anyone in the business world and is nearly legendary for building one of the world's largest and best computer manufacturing companies. Incredibly, it is a company he started in his college dorm room. Second, he is one of the wealthiest men in the country. Third, he is roughly our same age (ugh!). Finally, because of reasons one, two, and (especially) three, we knew there was a pretty good chance he had something to teach us.

Dell had articulated for us the exact reason our business was taking off.

We were right. At one point in the presentation, Mr. Dell showed a slide describing the Internet and the future of business. As he described the slide and gave industry predictions, we just about fell out of our seats! Without knowing we were in attendance, (or even knowing who we were), Dell had articulated for us the exact reason our business was taking off. We left the auditorium so excited that day we could have walked the eighty miles home instead of driving! What Dell described was an idea we could call the "three Cs."

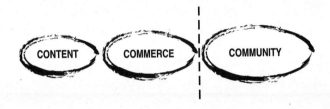

Content

The first "C", as shown in the diagram, stands for Content. As you can see, the first ellipse is the smallest and therefore the least important of the three. However, it is critical to Dell's explanation. His basic premise is that the Internet is the biggest trend of our lifetimes, and to build a business that doesn't have content on the World Wide Web is to miss the whole picture. Who wants to build in an industry that is flat and stale when an explosive trend is available? Who wants to be caught making vinyl records when compact discs come out? Who wants to be the leader in buggy technology when the automobile hits the scene?

This hit close to home for us. We had spent the years of our youth learning the details of automotive engineering, preparing for a career in big auto companies. But the auto industry, as exciting as it is (and as much as we love cars), is not an explosively growing industry. Each year in North America, the overall volume of new vehicles sold is pretty constant. The real battles are in the areas of technological advancement and carving out market share. The industry as a whole is pretty mature. The Internet world, though, is anything but mature! Think about it, whenever you have successful companies named "Yahoo!" you know the industry is a little immature! If it were mature, they would have called it "Yippee!" or "Splendid!"

Be involved where the action is: the Internet.

Sorry, you get the point! And we got Dell's point. Be involved where the action is: the Internet.

Dell went even further, however. Even more important than offering your content Online, which nearly everyone does these days, he emphasized that it had to be world-class, distinctive, and effective. To come to the marketplace with anything less than the best would be naïve. This is where the portfolio of LIFE products comes in. Organized into each of the 8 F categories, the LIFE business provides world-class, proven materials designed to change people's lives for the better. Have a struggling marriage? Dig into the Family category of products. Frustrated financially and sick of your consumer debt? Access the materials available in the Finances section, and so on. From audio to video training, from books to events, the LIFE business covers the entire spectrum of what's needed to improve one's life. (For the latest lineup of LIFE materials, see the Shopping Cart at www.the-life-business.com).

Commerce

The second "C" was Commerce. This represented financial transactions supporting product and service purchases, including customer service lines, product guarantees, shipping, tracking, compensation, and order fulfillment. Dell explained that it wasn't enough to have a presence on the Internet (Content). There are now millions and millions of Web sites, and anyone with a little computer savvy can create one entirely on his own. (The general rule is the younger someone is, the more likely he or she is able to do it!) Dell's point was that just having a Web site does not a company make. There are totally incompetent people out there hiding behind a Web site, trying to appear credible. It is important to have "bricks and mortar" to support the "clicks and orders."

Even more critical, though, and perhaps the biggest part of having "Commerce" right is compensation. For compensation to be correct it must be fair. Too often in the corporate world the pay goes to the wrong people. One reason there aren't Income Disclosure Statements available where most people work is because if there were, if everyone's incomes were disclosed publicly, there would be work stoppages. There might even be heart stoppages! This is because people would find out that things other than performance were being rewarded financially, such as seniority (perhaps the most common), nepotism (keeping it all in the family), favoritism, and any number of prejudices ranging from racism to age and gender discrimination.

With a compensation plan like that in the LIFE business, however, it is strict pay-for-performance. The pay plan is blind to age, color, or seniority. It only rewards results. Additionally, in the corporate world there is generally an unwritten agreement that an employee will be paid just enough to keep him or her from quitting. This agreement is acknowledged by workers who respond by doing just enough to keep from getting fired! Seriously, though, everyone knows that corporate compensations are generally stingy – the needs of the corporation coming ahead of those of the employee. It can sometimes be even worse in small business ownership, where the owner or entrepreneur is the last to get paid, if at all! But with the LIFE compensation plan, pay flows to the performer. And even better, the LIFE pay plan is extremely aggressive, offering the highest margin of "pay back" going out to the field to the people who are actually making things happen. (For more information on the LIFE compensation plan visit www.the-life-business.com and review the Income Disclosure Statement).

Community

It was the next circle or "C", which stands for Community that hit us like a bolt of lightening. In Dell's words, "The final stage is developing an online community." Anyone who styles hair for a living, runs a dental practice, or is in private legal practice already understands this concept, but to us, it was a revelation. What Dell meant by community was very similar to the word *clientele, but actually much, much more.*

The basic premise is as follows. We humans are habit-forming creatures. We naturally form habits that allow us to do things without thinking about them. Take the task of going to the grocery store to purchase our weekly food. After a while, how much thought do we really give this exercise? Do we survey the list of local grocery stores on a weekly basis deciding which will receive our business that week? Maybe. But more likely we get comfortable going someplace and after a while just start going there each time out of habit. You might say we get in a "groove" of buying our groceries at that particular store.

Take another example. Let's say it is Friday night and you and your spouse go out to dinner. It's been a long week and you're ready to relax, and besides, who wants to do dishes on Friday night? The question is: where do you go? Do you always try someplace new? Maybe once in a while. But if you're like most of us, you eventually start going to the same two or three "regular" restaurants that you both like. There may be 500 restaurants in your town, but you end up going only to two or three. Many times we even have a favorite section or booth! That's called being in a restaurant "groove." Let's do one more example. Growing up in an automotive town in an automotive area, it is no surprise that almost everybody we know loves cars. It is common to hear someone say something like, "I'm a Chevy man, always have been, always will be. My whole family is made up of Chevy people. My daddy was a Chevy guy, and his daddy before him. Guess my kids will all be Chevy people, too." Imagine how happy Chevrolet would be to hear such loyalty. Companies advertise, sure, to build an image and gain awareness, or maybe to announce the opening of a new store or to promote a sale item or two, but predominantly they thrive by developing a group of people who get in the habit of buying their goods or services. In effect, they work to build a group of people in a "groove" for their stuff. Dell very expertly called it a community.

Picture a big department store that moves into your town. Its owners buy a tract of land, clear all the trees, put up a big superstructure, pave a parking lot, paint the building and put up signs, fill it with inventory, hire two employees (joking), and open the doors for business. If it's a big name store, it probably doesn't need to do much more than announce its grand opening and customers come flocking in (assuming corporate headquarters has properly sized up the local demographics, etc.). They are counting on developing in that area a community of loyal, habitual customers for their store. If they can get you in there the first couple of times and make you like it, chances are you'll come back again and again. After a while, they won't have to advertise to you, you'll just come because you have become part of their community. This is how almost every business operates. Develop a loyal customer base that not only comes back again and again, but also tells a friend.

It all made sense to us. Many of you, as we stated earlier, are already familiar with the concept. It was what Dell explained next that was the point of all points. It was basically this: Building communities of loyal customers is fine and dandy in the physical world, but it is extremely difficult to build that kind of loyalty and habitual buying on the Internet. Whoever could figure that out, how to build a community of buyers loyal to an Internet business, would rule the Internet!

> *Whoever could figure that out, how to build a community of buyers loyal to an Internet business, would rule the Internet!*

We are paraphrasing, sure, but that's not to say we didn't want to sport little crowns on the way home! In summarizing his talk, Dell said, "As you look to harness the power of the Internet in your own business, focus on these three key areas: the online customer experience, which provides a strong and loyal base; rich content; high-value commerce that moves transactions to the Web to reduce costs dramatically; and bringing communities together to create a network with shared interests." We were immediately convinced then, and are even more so now, that Dell had described an enormous opportunity.

Connectedness

We like to think of the difference between a mere clientele and a true community as the difference between a group of satisfied customers and those who are downright amazed and astounded. One group is likely to come back again and again, but the other, the true community, is downright evangelical. This means they not only come back again and again, but they can't help but tell others the good news. Again, this is evident in the enthusiasm LIFE business build-

61

ers and customers express. For proof of this one need only attend a Team event where the LIFE business is being explained and promoted, or visit the LIFE website at www.the-life-business.com and click on Testimonials. People are "over the top" excited about the changes taking place in their lives through the 8 Fs of Faith, Family, Finances, Fitness, Following, Freedom, Friendship, and Fun. That's the power of community!

With the surge of Social Networking in our society it is evident that people are longing for a feeling of connectedness. With ever more means of communication, with an explosion of information and electronic noise, everyone is talking but nobody seems to be listening. We have grown more connected but at the same time more disconnected. We don't know our neighbors, but we'll spend hours online "chatting" with electronic "friends." More than ever there is the real need for the "high touch" to go along with the "high tech." People need real people in real relationships in real time. Building communities of people, actual communities where they meet and congregate, get together, share experiences, and forge real relationships, is more important today than ever. People yearn for this kind of connectedness to go along with all the electronic varieties. This is exactly where the Team system shines. Much more than a mere training system to help people build their LIFE business, the Team training system specializes in bringing people together in teams, where truly Together Everyone Achieves More.

The Hedgehog Concept

In his book *Good to Great,* Jim Collins talks about something called a "hedgehog" concept. It is the apex of all that a company does well, and is the core of what it exists to accomplish. It is the one thing in which it has the potential to be the best in the world. After listening to Dell, we knew clearly that what we had been helping people do to build their businesses was exactly in line with what he was teaching. Helping people build communities of people (who offer LIFE changing material to those in need) by helping them develop their leadership abilities is our hedgehog concept.

Helping people build communities of people (who offer LIFE changing material to those in need) by helping them develop their leadership abilities is our hedgehog concept.

In summary, the LIFE business provides the materials to change lives, the compensation to reward the performer and provide business ownership, and the Team training system provides the community to bring it all together. LIFE, it can be said, is a Team sport!

7
THE MASTER STRATEGY
TEAM APPROACH

Success is a decision, and growing a business does not happen by accident. One of our favorite sayings is, "Victory occurs only by design." There is no such thing as luck. If there were, it would be an acronym for "Laboring Under Correct Knowledge." William Jennings Bryant said, "Destiny is not a matter of chance, it is a matter of choice. It is not something to be waited for, but, rather, something to be achieved."

Some people think that if they work hard long enough they will achieve success, which simply isn't true. This false notion might be based upon a common saying that unfortunately is only a partial truth: "hard work is the key to success." We don't think anyone who has accomplished great things in life will deny that a lot of hard work and effort was required along the way. However, hard work is not the key, but only a component of success. Smart work combined with hard work over time is what produces results.

> *Smart work combined with hard work, over time, is what produces results.*

Victory by Design doesn't simply mean it is intentional, as when someone accomplishes a goal for which he or she has long been striving. It also means the path to success is scripted and calculated, that all the efforts toward the goal are expended with a specific intent.

Let's take the statue of David as an example. It is known throughout the world as a masterpiece. Michelangelo was a master sculptor and turned a discarded chunk of marble into one of the most valuable statues of all time. To suggest that he accomplished it through hard work would not be totally wrong. Certainly, it took time and effort. Sculpting is physical work and not easy. However, this is not the whole story. You see, whenever someone thinks that hard work leads to success, it's like suggesting that all Michelangelo did was walk up to a piece of marble and start chipping away. He just hammered on that chisel 4,692 times, and wham, there was David, standing there stark naked! Anybody who duplicates that amount of effort should be able to duplicate the results, right? Obviously not. Michelangelo had to force that statue to appear out of that stone. It became David only by design.

While it's likely that nobody reading this book has the artistic talent of a Michelangelo, in the business world we can apply the principle of Victory by Design to force our own version of success. To achieve something significant requires a plan. There must be a strategy. It must be specific, focused, and scripted. Michelangelo

> *"A mature business knows how it got to be where it is, and what it must do to get where it wants to go."*
>
> -Michael Gerber

Gerber says, "A mature business knows how it got to be where it is, and what it must do to get where it wants to go."

Our biggest challenge in the beginning was learning this exact lesson. We were willing to work hard, and we did. It was hard work that had gotten us college degrees and early success in corporate America, but things didn't take off (and the Team really wasn't even formed) until we learned to put the work-smart with the work hard.

A Little Background

In a simplified sense, companies can increase earnings three ways:

1. By raising prices
2. By lowering costs
3. By expanding

Raising prices is very difficult. Customers want lower prices, not higher. Besides, if prices are increased, there is always competition willing to charge less and take that market share. So this is not a viable option in most situations.

Lowering costs is a worthy objective for any company. Entire industries exist for the sole purpose of helping companies become more efficient by lowering the costs of doing business. Value engineering takes unnecessary costs out of product designs, and lean manufacturing techniques optimize the production process and its costs. Consultants and college courses are geared toward cost reduction; but even while cost reduction is an obvious objective, it is not easy, and in many cases can be taken too far. Customers don't want products of lower quality, and employees don't like working for less pay. In most cases, if cost reduction were the only way a company could do better financially they would be stuck.

Expansion is, in fact, the best way a company can make more money. Noel Tichy and Ram Charan wrote a whole book dedicated to the subject, entitled *Every Business is a Growth Business.* That title says it all. By increasing revenues, a company can enjoy greater economies of scale, can invest more in future projects, and can usually experience higher profits. In fact, most serious stock investors agree that a key indicator for analyzing companies is something called "projected earnings growth." It is not enough to know where a given company is in the moment; what's really important is its growth potential in the future. Michael Gerber says, "The natural disposition of every business is to either grow or contract." Tichy says, "The true measure of a leader is whether he or she has made the assets under their control more valuable today than they were yesterday." That's growth. The Team training system is no different. We knew that to help people develop viable businesses we had to help them grow. We also (eventually) learned that growth wouldn't just happen because people were working hard. We needed a strategy. We needed a specific plan for growth.

Finding the Right People

James Buchanan Duke, the founder of American Tobacco Company, which grew into one of the biggest conglomerates in the world, said, "A man's most valuable capital is the men he picks out to work with him." Ross Perot, founder of EDS and Perot Systems, said, "Our highest priority was to attract great people. I spent a lot of time recruiting. Your success will be based on your judgment in building a great team of people."

> *"Our highest priority was to attract great people... Your success will be based on your judgment in building a great team of people."*
> -Ross Perot

We came to the realization that if the Team was going to enable people to reach their full potential, it would need to find the right kind of people to get involved. It would need to find and develop leaders. John Maxwell in *The 21 Irrefutable Laws of Leadership* says, "Everything rises and falls on leadership."

Eventually, we boiled it down to four traits that embody what the Team encourages people to look for when expanding their business, namely, people who are:

1. Ambitious
2. Looking
3. Teachable
4. Honest

Whenever these four attributes are true of someone, that person is a good fit for someone as a new LIFE business partner.

The first thing we teach people to look for is someone who is "ambitious." Without it, success just won't happen. In his book, *Made in America*, Sam Walton gives a list of his 10 rules for business success, but before even starting the list, he said, "I do seem to have a couple dozen things that I've singled out at one time or another as the 'key' to the whole thing. One I don't even have on my list is 'work hard.' If you don't know that already, or you're not willing to do it, you probably won't be going far enough to need my list anyway." We love that! Talk about a straight shooter! Hard work is not the lone ingredient in success, but it is one of the prerequisites. We often say that business is not for everybody, and one of the reasons is because not everybody is ambitious. Think about where you work. Is there anybody there who wouldn't qualify to be called "ambitious"? We thought so.

The second thing we teach people to look for is someone who is "looking" for a better life. It might be more pay, better security, a chance to get out of debt, more status, time with family, travel, toys, or just freedom to make choices not currently available. However, it is an absolute must that someone possesses the desire for a better future. Without that desire, they just aren't "looking" and they won't make it. Again, you can quickly see that this eliminates some people. Plenty of people out there are ambitious, but some are doing exactly what they want to do already. Through speaking to large audiences over the years, we have noticed something interesting: after a while things kind of average out. We have asked audiences throughout the nation to raise their hands if they would quit their current jobs if money were no object. The number of people who have raised their hands is consistently around 80 percent of the crowd. Most of the rest say they would do less of their current job, but keep doing a little bit of it on their terms. A very select few state that they love what they do and would therefore do it for free.

The third trait is that someone must be "teachable." There are many people who are ambitious, and about eighty percent of these are looking for better opportunities in life, but we lose another group when we say they also need to be teachable. There are people out there whose skin has grown right over their ears. They can't listen to anything you say, especially if you have something to teach them. They know everything about everything, and they even know what they don't know (just ask them). If success is like walking through a minefield, and the best way through is to follow someone who has made it across, it would be a good idea to listen to that person. One of Team's favorite sayings is that, "If you're too big to follow, you're too small to lead." Becoming a student instead of a critic or know-it-all is one of the key attitudes for success. These traits apply in any field where reward is based upon merit.

"If you're too big to follow, you're too small to lead."

The final aspect is that the person be "honest." This should go without saying, but our experience has been that there are a lot of people out there who suffer from SFN disease, caused by the deadly Something-For-Nothing virus. They take shortcuts and misrepresent things and operate without integrity. While some may think they can get ahead by being untruthful, eventually the truth comes out. Long term, it always catches up with them. To be a leader requires integrity and character. John Morley said, "No man can climb out beyond the limitations of his own character."

Formation of Team Approach

In the early days, before we had really been able to help people get their businesses moving, we knew the goal was to develop consistent, ongoing, explosive growth. We realized we were helping people search for people of the caliber just described. The problem was that we didn't know how to help them find them. More accurately, we didn't have a systematic way of helping people find them. We had learned that without a system we would have nothing but chaos, and that's exactly what it felt like.

The breakthrough came when we realized how differently people reacted to seeing a business plan. These reactions could basically be broken into four categories:

Not looking

Not Sure

Maybe Looking

Seriously Looking

71

We realized the need to design a system that would provide something for each of these categories. Until that point in time, our approach was aimed only at helping people find superstar performers right out of the box. We were ignoring the fact that many others came into a business with less initial inclination. Looking back now, it's amazing we had helped anyone experience even a limited amount of success. We were trying to shove a bunch of round pegs in square holes.

It came down to differing levels of interest and proficiency. Eventually, we learned that people needed to have an apprenticeship process where they could gain experience and develop the skill sets required for building a business. We discovered that nobody comes into the business fully trained. Sure they have skills and talents, but core competencies still need to be developed. To accomplish this, the Team focuses on helping people learn to "teach by showing." Audio recordings and books develop the theory, meetings give firsthand training, but the actual hands-on learning is what brings it together. Once someone develops basic proficiencies, he or she is then more capable to step out and take a leadership role in the development of his or her business.

These ideas were pared with the concept of depth, in which people work together to build teams of business owners. It's all based on relationships, and could be described fairly accurately by Dell's term "Direct Relationship Marketing." Its interconnectedness provides some of the benefits of franchising, as well.

To see why catering to varied levels of interest and focusing on building teams as an apprenticeship process is so effective, let's look once again at the four reactions of people to the LIFE business plan. It is obvious that each person's reaction requires a different startup procedure. They can all join the LIFE business, but follow different paths. Their levels of activity and training are specifically matched to their degree of interest, but all get to work within a team. This gives each a chance to learn by becoming involved and experiencing some progress, but simultaneously allows them participation at their own pace. Before we discovered this, the only type of person for which we had a program was the one shown at the bottom of the illustration - the most committed and eager. Now there is room for everybody. In this system, there is no something-for-nothing, but there is something for everyone!

It is beyond the scope of this book to delve too deeply into the details of building depth and the apprenticeship process, but suffice it to say that the results have been astounding. We have learned, and are continuing to learn, the old axiom that "individuals can flourish, but teams can explode."

8
GENERATING VOLUME
CUSTOMERS AND SUBSCRIPTIONS

Getting started with any business is a process. *Information* from the Team's training system teaches the new LIFE member about his or her business in terms of principles and specifics, answers his or her questions, and sets him or her on the path to success. But information by itself can only do so much. What is needed next to reinforce that information is *progress*. To learn something new is one thing, to see it demonstrated is quite another. Progress accomplishes that. The master strategy we talked about in Chapter 7, Team Approach, provides the progress that demonstrates to the new LIFE member that the business works and that he or she can do it! Even so, there is still more reinforcement available, and that is the earning of *income*. Information is great, progress is great, but income completes the picture. After all, the measure of a business is how well it is able to generate income for its owner(s), and some businesses are more profitable than others. The diagram looks like this:

INFORMATION, PROGRESS, INCOME

EXCITEMENT AND BELIEF

Since learning and progress will continue as income builds, which will then lead to more learning and more progress, and then still more income, the diagram might be more accurately represented as shown below:

Becoming Your Own Best Customer

When it comes to generating income, the key point to remember is that when the products flow the money flows. Those who learn how to generate a large amount of movement of LIFE changing materials into the lives of people in need will be a long way down the road toward making a large income through the LIFE business. And, the best way to convince others of the viability of the LIFE materials for improving their own lives is to be convinced yourself. Abraham Lincoln was quoted as saying, "Example is not the main thing in influencing other people; it's the only thing." Leadership expert John Maxwell wrote, "The most valuable gift a leader can give is being a good example."

Personal testimony is one of the most powerful forms of advertising, as we've already discussed. Think about the last hit movie you saw at the theater. Did you go see it because of an advertisement? Or was it more likely that you risked the time and money to see it based upon the recommendation of someone else, perhaps a trusted friend or relative? This is called word-of-mouth marketing, and no matter the sophistication of technology in the world, word-of-mouth is still one of the most effective forms of advertising. In relationship marketing strategies, word-of-mouth becomes a powerful force for building an ongoing clientele of customers. The strategy is to find and satisfy a consistent group of customers, who, of course, become so excited by the product you provide them (shipped to their door automatically without any "heavy lifting" by you) that they recommend other customers too. This is the foundation of the healthiest and most profitable type of business.

> *In relationship marketing strategies, word-of-mouth becomes a powerful force for building an ongoing clientele of customers.*

When it comes to owning a business that makes money by moving information through a community, it only stands to reason then that the example of the LIFE member will be a large part of his or her success with customers. What we are talking about here is becoming an expert on the products that will be marketed. The best way to do this is to become a dedicated consumer of them yourself. Becoming your own best customer will increase your enthusiasm, expertise, and experience with the product and will make it much easier to represent to customers. When someone is having difficulty in their marriage, you will know just which CD pack to hand them. Likewise, when someone is hurting financially, you will be familiar with the best LIFE materials for their particular situation. The same holds true for any of the 8 Fs. For a business owner to maximize his or her success, utilizing one's own products on a regular basis is the only place to start!

Developing a Clientele

One is not in business, however, if all one does is use one's own product. For money to be made, a solid business must find, attract, and keep customers who buy the product even though they may have no interest in becoming involved in the business that markets the product.

The best way to generate retail profits, ready income, and ongoing volume is to establish a solid customer base. This will most likely be comprised of both one-time sales and subscribing customers. Again, the best way to start this process is to be familiar with the products yourself and have enough on hand to sample and sell. The business owner who doesn't have products on hand to sell is already out of business! When a business owner samples his/her products to prospective buyers, it generates conversations, contacts, and sales.

Some people get nervous when the word 'sales' is mentioned. This is unfounded. With LIFE, sharing the product is all that's necessary to determine if someone is interested in purchasing some for themselves. The CDs are very entertaining, the books are fun and interesting, and the events are a blast - all this in addition to being extremely relevant to living a better life. So "sales" is often the result of loaning someone a CD, book, or getting them to an event, at which point they decide to purchase materials or subscribe to them for themselves. It's that easy. We are in the Information Age, and all the LIFE member does is merely make relevant information available to those in need.

Subscriptions

Which brings us to a very important point. The bread and butter of the product offerings are the *subscriptions*. At the time of this writing, LIFE offers three distinct subscriptions:

1. The LIFE series – dedicated to all 8 Fs
2. The LLR (Launching a Leadership Revolution) series – dedicated to helping people grow in their leadership ability
3. The AGO (All Grace Outreach) series – dedicated to helping people grow spiritually

Customers (and certainly members) may subscribe to any of these, all of them, or any two in combination. By connecting customers with the appropriate subscription package(s), the LIFE member is beginning a process that will be much more likely to bring lasting change to the customer's life than a mere CD or book could accomplish. With the power of an ongoing supply of timeless truth the customer can find reinforcement over time – one of the key strategies for lasting personal change. Never underestimate the power of repetition and ongoing inputs to bring about change in someone's life - in fact, it is one of the only methods that truly can.

The other benefit of subscriptions, is that the customer volume is steady and ongoing. One can build a business of product flow that grows over time. All professional LIFE members treat subscriptions as one of their key business strategies, getting on it themselves and helping their customers to do the same.

3 for Free

While the benefits of being on a subscription are for both LIFE members and customers, there is another exciting program available to both customers and members. This enlists the customer to help in building the LIFE member's business. Here's how it works:

As a customer or member subscribes to one, two or three of the packages listed above, he or she is given the further incentive to attract other customers who do the same. Once that customer or member signs up three or more customers on equivalent or greater dollar value subscriptions, his subscription will be free the next month.

This is a beautiful program for both customer and LIFE member because the customer gets a 100% discount and the LIFE member gets growth in volume without having to do it himself. (Please see www.the-life-business.com for more information on the 3 for Free program).

9

TARGETING SUCCESS

THE LEADERSHIP REVOLUTION

Operating at the intersection of four exciting industries puts people in a position to win. Discovering the master strategy of Team Approach was the inertia that got the train moving. Operating in one of the hottest consumer markets – leveraging information - provided massive momentum. But the train still needs a track to run on. Even Dell said, "A brilliant business model alone doesn't create a sustainable advantage."

> *"A brilliant business model alone doesn't create a sustainable advantage."*
> -Michael Dell

We knew there would be no free lunch. We had to learn to help people drive this thing. And we had to get good at developing others that could do the same thing. It wasn't enough to become leaders ourselves. It wouldn't even be enough to learn to develop other leaders. To grow at the rate of our potential, we would need to develop leaders that were capable of developing other leaders. This is what Jim Collins in the book *Good to Great* calls "Level 5 Leadership," and he wrote an entire book to show how crucial it is in becoming not just a "good" business but also a "great" one.

In order to fulfill the potential of the LIFE business and the impact it can make in people's lives, we need to foster massive growth in leadership capability. Even though we've been talking about individual business heroes throughout this book like Walton and Dell and Kroc, these men did not do it alone. In fact, all of them would go to great lengths to explain that they had world-class help as a major factor in their success. The Team story is no exception. We know that as we pursue our vision for the future, we will need to help people develop even more talent in their "leadership bullpen." That is what we call the "Leadership Revolution" that powers the LIFE business.

Vision

Vision is tomorrow's reality expressed as an idea today. "Without a vision, the people

Vision is tomorrow's reality expressed as an idea today.

will perish," says the Bible. "If you aim at nothing you'll hit it with amazing accuracy," goes another saying. "Many have sight, but only a few have vision." "Everyone ends up somewhere in life, but a few people end up somewhere on purpose." In *Visioneering* Andy Stanley describes the culmination of one of the world's most revolutionary visions:

"On December 17, 1903, at 10:35 A.M., Orville Wright secured his place in history by executing the first powered and sustained flight from level ground. For twelve gravity-defying seconds he flew 120 feet along the dunes of the Outer Banks of North Carolina.

In the field of aviation, his historic event represents a beginning. But for Orville and Wilbur Wright, it was the end of a long and tedious journey. A journey initiated by a dream common to every little boy - the desire to fly. But what most children abandon to the domain of fantasy, Orville and Wilbur Wright seized upon as potential reality. They believed they could fly. More than that, they believed they should fly."

What the Wright brothers accomplished that morning was not the result of luck or chance or being in the right place at the right time. It was the direct result of a vision they had sought since they were little boys playing with paper toys. Stanley says that visions evoke passion, provide motivation, give clear direction, and develop purpose.

It is widely known that having a clear vision is fundamental to good leadership. The Team's vision is to help one million people be in business for themselves, and to change the way information marketing is done in the world to the benefit of the LIFE member and the consumer. Further, each LIFE member develops his own individual vision for where his business can take him in life. As a team, we couldn't agree more with the Chinese Proverb that states:

If your vision is for a year, plant wheat.
If your vision is for ten years, plant trees.
If your vision is for a lifetime, plant people.

Mission

True leaders are motivated by much more than money or material reward. At some point, it has to become a passion. The Team's mission is to help people "Have Fun, Make Money, and Make a Difference."

Let's start with "Have Fun." We have never been ones to take ourselves too seriously.

Let's face it, too many people are involved in careers where they might be doing okay financially, but they can't stand what they do. At the Team, we want to be sure we start out by helping people enjoy the journey. As Bill George, former chairman and CEO of Medtronic, the world's leading medical technology company says, "The journey itself is the message." You may as well enjoy it.

Second comes "Make Money." Although business can be a lot of fun, we don't want to stop at fun. LIFE is a premier opportunity for financial reward.

Money is the scorecard of business; it is the scoreboard or the report card. The way the LIFE compensation plan is structured, money becomes the direct result of serving other people. The more you serve, the more you deserve. We don't promote nor condone the pursuit of money for the sake of trappings or materialism, but we do get excited about the good things money can do in the hands of good people. There is plenty of financial reward to be gained by the proper building of the LIFE business. Some would choose to get out of debt, retire early from their jobs, bring their wives home from work to raise young children, buy cars and special trips for parents and grandparents, and send in-laws on slow, slow cruises around the world.

Yes there is money to be earned in business, and it is fun when it starts to roll in, but after a while, money loses its sting. Once you dig out of debt, accumulate some toys and a nice house; you actually start looking deeper (if you hadn't already). That's where the third part of the mission, "Make a Difference," comes in. The Team's mission involves the desire to impact the lives of people in a positive way, and in doing so, help people achieve success that transcends material accomplishment and leads to significance. Every time a LIFE member offers someone a chance, and thereby hope, he or she is opening the door to making a positive impact in that person's life. By partnering and leading, he or she can bring it to fruition. Helping people to help people: that's making a difference one person at a time.

The Team's mission involves the desire to impact the lives of people in a positive way, and in doing so, achieve success that transcends material accomplishment and leads to significance.

We had never before in life had the opportunity to "Have Fun, Make Money, and Make a Difference" simultaneously. Where else could we have this much fun, make this kind of money, and see such a positive impact on people's lives on a daily basis? It may exist out there, and maybe you experience it in your work life right now, but what many people have found is that, for them, it was only to be found by participating in the LIFE business.

Purpose

Having a vision and a mission to bring that vision to reality are nothing if not driven by a purpose. It's called leading with the heart. Bill George says, "When [people have] a deeper purpose, their results will vastly exceed those who use only their minds and their bodies." Before his leadership had a purpose, George said his abilities "hit a wall. Sure, I was leading, but the purpose of my efforts was not at all clear. Where was my leading leading to?"

Kevin and Jackie Freiberg, in their book *Nuts!* written about Southwest Airlines, the most consistently profitable airline in the country, said "People are drawn to Southwest Airlines because, intuitively or otherwise, they want to be part of a cause that gives them a sense of meaning and significance; they want to belong to something larger than themselves. Ron Ricks, Southwest's vice president of governmental affairs, often invokes a slogan Southwest people hold dear: It's not a job, it's a crusade." One of Team's often-quoted statements is that "This is our chance to do something special."

The Team's purpose is to make a difference in culture and in the individual lives of LIFE customers. Noel Tichy said "We must have world-class leaders with unyielding integrity who will transform their organizations and develop a new generation of leaders.

Without such leadership, our free-enterprise society is undermined." Many of the supports of free enterprise and the right to build a business and earn a profit are under attack in our entitlement society. There are cracks in the foundations of our freedom that our founding fathers did not intend nor foresee. There are tears in the fabric of the character of our nation that left unrepaired, threaten our individual freedoms. Charles Crismier said, "America has now reached the point where it permits almost everything and stands for nothing." By lifting up example after example of individual business success for people of all ages, races, genders, and social classifications, we can make a strong statement for the power of the individual and the ability of groups of people working together. By contributing to the well being of our economic system, we preserve the freedoms we have enjoyed for those who are to follow. It's not just about winning or accomplishing, it's also about giving. As Albert Schweitzer said, "We make a living by what we get, but we make a life by what we give."

> *"We must have world-class leaders with unyielding integrity who will transform their organizations and develop a new generation of leaders. Without such leadership, our free-enterprise society is undermined."*
>
> -Noel Tichy

Dreams

In the tale of *Alice in Wonderland*, Alice comes to a fork in the road and asks the cat in the nearby tree which road she should take. When the cat asks, "Do you know where you want to go?" Alice answers, "No." To which the cat replies, "Then any road will get you there."

Without a vision, a mission, and a purpose, leadership is hollow and short-lived. But just as important, and especially on an individual basis, dreams of a better future are critically necessary. We remember hearing that the "facts don't count if you dream a big enough dream," and thinking that such talk was fantasyland stuff. After all, we were from corporate America; nobody talks about "dreams." You might talk about goals or objectives, but dreams? Come on.

John Eldredge, the author of *Wild at Heart,* says that hardwired into every man is the burning desire for three things:

1. A battle to fight
2. An adventure to live
3. A beauty to win

In our experience, the term "dream" incorporates these three precepts into one.

What does he mean by a "battle to fight?" Aren't we talking about business here? Of course, but anybody who has pursued something with all their might, who has tried to create a successful business and radically change their financial situation, doesn't have to look very hard to see the similarities to a battle. In fact, George Eastman, the founder of Eastman Kodak Co. said, "Peace . . . extends only to private life. In business it is war all the time." We like that.

The reason building a business or chasing your career or anything of the sort feels like a battle is that the status quo is firmly entrenched. Team likes to say, "Goals are a planned assault on the status quo." Nothing happens automatically, it has to be forced, and one has to battle one's way there. It is because the status quo, "getting by," to continue doing the same old thing and getting the same old results, requires nothing of you. To advance, to grow, to improve, to create, requires change and growth. One must step out of the comfort zone and run against the grain. That takes effort. It is a fight. However like any worthwhile challenge, it is a fight that brings great rewards. Those rewards are what we refer to as "dreams."

To build a business that focuses on helping people accomplish their financial goals and dreams in life is a special kind of reward all in itself. But it is not easy, automatic, or overnight. That is why dreams are so important.

"Goals are a planned assault on the status quo."

The lure of a better tomorrow and the rewards of accomplishment are necessary to pull one ahead into the battle.

All through the journey so far we have been driven by dreams. We wanted better homes and nicer cars. We wanted to get out of debt. We wanted flexibility in our schedules and to be in charge of how much we could earn. We wanted our wives to have the option of staying home with the kids. We wanted to give more to church and charities like the M.O.R.E. Project and leave a financial legacy that would outlast us. We wanted to get the "money monkey" off our backs. These are dreams; probably similar to the dreams of most ambitious people. Dreams like these are required to fuel a business to higher and higher levels. For anyone to make it big, they too, will need to be driven by dreams.

All dreams, however, aren't material dreams. The second aspect Eldredge writes about is "an adventure to live." Who doesn't want to have an adventurous life? Who doesn't like to see and experience new things, develop new relationships and discover and learn things previously unfamiliar? Who wouldn't like to take up golf or learn to sail or go camping for the first time or take flying lessons? Tasting new foods, seeing unfamiliar places, hearing new sounds and seeing new sites is all very rewarding and stimulating; it becomes part of the "spice of life." The desire to have some adventure in your life is another type of dream, what might be called an "action dream" or a dream to "experience." Paradoxically, the very building of a business can become an adventure in itself. What begins as a means to obtain dreams can turn into a dream activity itself! Talk about rewarding. We can think of no bigger adventure to live than creating something that matters. Every LIFE member who expends energy to create his or her business is living an adventure.

In the third dream, to have "a beauty to win," Eldredge refers mostly to lifelong companionship. Romantic aspects aside, though, we believe it's a deep desire for people to be appreciated and to be part of the lives of other people that matter. It's the concept of connectedness we've been discussing throughout this book. We want the approval from those we respect. We want to know that we are important and we are worthy of their recognition.

In helping LIFE members, one of the biggest dreams that have come true and continue to do so on a daily basis is something called camaraderie. These past years we have been blessed with associating with leaders that are second to none. Relationships with quality people and deep friendships are forged for a lifetime. Having a common purpose in life, striving for great accomplishment alongside one another, and building lasting bonds while doing it, has been one of our biggest dreams come true. Anybody aspiring to accomplishment in LIFE operates in a positive environment of support and encouragement, in which some of the deepest and most lasting friendships will be born. This is the kind of thing that happens when people engage in a battle for greatness, together.

So whether dreams are of a material nature, or for adventure or camaraderie, in the LIFE business we specialize in enabling people to make them come true. As we've heard it said, "You have to have a dream in order to have a dream come true." Yes Alice, you need to know where you are going!

Commitment

The final piece of the recipe is commitment. Goethe said, "The moment one definitely commits oneself, then providence moves too. All sorts of things occur to help that would never otherwise have occurred . . . Whatever you can do or dream you can, begin it. Boldness has genius, power and magic in it." Commitment smoothes things out and brings achievement into focus. We call it "LIFE in the zone." John Maxwell says, "Leaders find a way to win. Victorious leaders share an inability to accept defeat."

"Leaders find a way to win. Victorious leaders share an inability to accept defeat."
-John Maxwell

Our experience has been that many people do just enough not to make it. They will go part of the way, but not follow through. They'll do a few initial steps, but won't complete things. It's a lot easier to find "starters" than "finishers." We seem to be a continent made up of starters, but finishers are rare. Success is not normally complicated. It is usually a matter of hanging on long after everybody else has let go.

There is a famous legend about a gold miner who dug into the side of a certain mountain range for 20 years. He dug hundreds of shafts, but after penetrating a little way with each would start anew someplace else. Each time, he would tell his friends he was just about to hit pay dirt. As he grew older, he became frustrated, eventually died penniless, never making his big score. After his death the group that gained access to his mountain continued digging a few of the shafts he'd started, and within weeks hit one of the biggest veins of gold found to date in North America. The saddest detail of the story is that they only had to dig three feet deeper. Just three more feet!

We see people like that enter the world of business all the time. They do some work, apply themselves a little, and then they move on to something else just before they would have experienced progress. Normally people just get distracted. One of the objectives of both the LIFE materials and the TEAM training system is to provide constant inputs to people so they will stay the course and remain focused. It's amazing how little is required to distract some people. Have you ever watched a bunch of five year olds learning to play T-ball? They get placed out on the field, six or eight outfielders included. The game starts, and by the time the first ball is hit (two feet or so), half of the kids are chasing butterflies, picking worms up off the ground or lying on their backs finding pictures in the clouds. It's funny, but we see grown adults act like that in their businesses. Things will be going great and then suddenly some miniscule thing in life distracts them. H. Ross Perot says, "Most of us quit at the one-yard line." Abraham Lincoln said, "Always bear in mind that your own resolution to succeed is more important than any other thing."

Commitment means victory is the only option. Success requires focus. Focus comes from having vision and a mission, living with a purpose and pursuing worthwhile dreams and goals. The LIFE materials and Team training system are designed to enhance commitment and help people maintain focus as they build their businesses. The LIFE business doesn't require special talents or gifts at birth. Everything it takes is based on skills. Skills can be learned. But they also have to be applied. Success will come to those who get committed and stay the course. And many times, it's just three more feet!

Our training system and mentoring process is designed to build commitment and help people maintain focus as they build their businesses.

LIFE is ultimately about involving people in a chance to make a difference. One of our favorite anonymous quotes goes like this:

"Leadership is the practice of helping people see and then contribute to leaving the world a better place than the way they found it."

10
Swimming Up Stream
Dream, Struggle, Victory

Maury Klein in his book, *The Change Makers,* said "The process of discovery must always swim against the powerful tide of conventional wisdom." We were surprised at people's reactions when we decided to leave our corporate jobs to build businesses full time. We had prepared financially, the businesses and incomes were growing, and it was a calculated financial move. We would never encourage anybody to put their current income in jeopardy because they are excited about what they can accomplish in the LIFE business. Rather, what we teach is to "earn your way out." Build your LIFE business, make some money, get out of debt, and then consider your alternatives. We took our own advice, of course, and were prepared. But that didn't silence the skeptics. "What are you guys doing? Are you sure? Boy, we'd hate to see you get hurt. What about all your college degrees?"

These were in many cases sincere questions of concern. But people just didn't understand. They didn't see what we saw. In the previous chapter we talked about having a dream and a purpose that will drive you forward in building your LIFE business. We liken it to the analogy of a dog running loose in the back yard that spots a squirrel on the ground. Any dog worth his salt will take off with everything in his being to catch that squirrel. You can readily picture the scene: Little Spike tears off with wheels spinning, grass shooting up behind as he focuses in on the squirrel with laser precision. The squirrel realizes his peril and hauls fur to the nearest tree trunk. Spike changes direction and lets out a little snarl, real tough-like, and finds yet another gear. The chase is really on now as the squirrel is cut off from his escape but bolts off at a ninety before Spike can put on the brakes. Spike hits the tree, bounces off, snarls again and makes a bee-line for the squirrel that is now heading toward the telephone pole. Let's break into the action right there. Anyone reading this has probably witnessed a similar scene. Watching it unfold, the behavior of Spike is no great mystery; everybody knows that dogs love to chase squirrels. ("Why?" is another question. Maybe the squirrel species did something unthinkable to a pack of Chihuahuas way back in some previous age. We don't know.) The point is that the behavior of the dog is explained by seeing the squirrel. Now imagine if we eliminated the squirrel from this scene and re-played it. Spike races all over the back yard chasing and snarling at nothing, as far as we can see. Many people building the LIFE business come to realize they are chasing after something others just can't see. Of course they look a little half-baked in other's eyes because others can't see their squirrel. They just can't see what is being chased!

Expect Resistance

Learning to expect resistance is an important lesson. When you decide to step out and pursue success, in anything, there will be detractors. There will be people who shine doubt on what you are doing. As a matter of fact, negative resistance will be inversely proportional to the size of the undertaking: the bigger the dream, the bigger the

"Great spirits have always encountered violent opposition from mediocre minds."
-Albert Einstein

critics. It was Albert Einstein who said, "Great spirits have always encountered violent opposition from mediocre minds."

Sam Walton said his Rule #10 was to "Swim upstream. Go the other way. Ignore the conventional wisdom. Be prepared for a lot of folks to wave you down and tell you you're headed the wrong way."

There are really three classes of critics, those who react negatively to your dreams and aspirations:

1. Out of sincere concern for your well being,
2. Out of jealousy or envy, or
3. Out of hatred for the very idea of what you are trying to accomplish.

The key to finding success in life is to focus on what you know is right and ignore the negatives that come up along the way. The higher you want to climb the ladder of success, the more your butt will be showing above the crowd. You can expect to get hit with a tomato or two.

The key to finding success in life is to focus on what you know is right and ignore the negatives that come up along the way.

For those who have a legitimate interest in your well-being and sincerely care about you, simply explain your position and help them, as best you can, to see the "squirrel." They may or may not see it, but if they are real friends, they will support you even if they disagree with your judgment.

The second category of people, those who are jealous or uneasy with your success, will be plentiful. Smile, love them where they are in life, pray for them, and hold your tongue. There is a famous saying that people want to see you get by, just not by *them*. There is another cute analogy based on biological fact. Blue crabs are fully capable of climbing out of a five-gallon

95

bucket. Put two blue crabs together in a bucket and they will both not only remain inside the bucket but also stay until they die. This is because one crab will pull the other one down if it starts to climb out, and vise versa. In many ways, we see people behave this way when forced to observe the success of somebody else.

Andy Stanley in the book *Visioneering* said "When someone catches a vision for bettering himself educationally or financially, his vision is often met with criticism from the people closest to him. Why? Because those who have no vision for their own academic pursuits or financial freedom feel threatened by those who have decided to get up and do something with themselves. Their insecurities about their own lack of education surface or they are forced to take a painful look at where they are financially as opposed to where they could be."

The final category of critics really makes life interesting. Believe it or not, some are staunchly opposed to almost everything you hold dear in life. If you are for freedom, there are those who want to take it away. If you believe in saluting the flag, there are those who want to burn it. The list goes on indefinitely. This is where success becomes a battle - because to create anything, to take a stand on anything, requires change, and we already mentioned that the only people who like changes are babies!

Critics Are Wrong

While the peanut gallery is busy saying something can't be done, a few leaders with courage are busy doing it.

The simplest way to overcome these obstacles is to realize that critics are cowards. Critics are spectators. Criticism is the death-gurgle of a non-achiever. While the peanut gallery is busy saying something can't be done, a few

96

leaders with courage are busy doing it. They said if man was meant to fly, God would have given him wings, but airplanes are a way of life today. They said that cars were run by "infernal combustion" and were a fad, but they are indispensable to our modern way of life. They said we could never put a man on the moon, but that was done three and a half decades ago (and, incredibly, twenty years before anyone thought to put wheels on luggage). Usually when "they" say something cannot be done a daring leader somewhere is dreaming of that very thing and making it a reality.

F. A. Hayek said, "Nothing is more securely lodged than the ignorance of the experts." Look at some of these famous critiques that were proven embarrassingly wrong, as detailed in the book Wrong! by Jane O'Boyle:

- "Hurrah, boys, we've got them! We'll finish them up and then go home to our station." – General George Custer, when first sighting a Sioux encampment near the Little Big Horn, 1876.
- "People will tire of talkers. Talking is no substitute for the good acting we had in silent pictures." – Thomas Edison, 1925, on new movies with sound.
- "Drill for oil? You mean, drill into the ground to try to find oil? You're crazy." – Professional drillers in 1859, when Edwin Drake tried to enlist their services.
- "The telephone has too many shortcomings to be seriously considered as a means of communication. The device is inherently of no value to us." – Western Union internal memo, 1876.
- "Everything that can be invented, has been invented." – Charles Duell, commissioner of U.S. Patent Office, 1899.
- "I think there is a world market for maybe five computers." – Thomas Watson, IBM chairman, 1943.

- "There is no reason anyone would ever want a computer in their home." – Ken Olsen, president, CEO, and founder of Digital Equipment, 1977.
- "Stocks have reached what looks like a permanently high plateau." – Irving Fisher, Yale University Professor of economics, October 17, 1929.
- "The concept is interesting and well-formed, but in order to earn better than a 'C', the idea must be feasible." – A business professor at Yale University in 1966, on Fred Smith's senior thesis outlining a reliable overnight delivery service. Smith later founded Federal Express.
- "The Internet will collapse within a year." – Bob Metcalf, founder of 3Com Corporation, 1995.

Building the LIFE business has been no different. Every step of the way, with every innovation and advancement, there were those saying it couldn't be done, or that it had already been tried, or that it wasn't legal, or something or other. Kevin and Jackie Freiberg said, "There will always be those who lounge in the safety of convention, who criticize you for daring to live life authentically in order to justify themselves. These are the same people who are off seeking permission while the rest of us are pursuing our dreams." According to Don Soderquist of Wal-Mart, "As with all people who are successful, [Abraham] Lincoln said, you don't pull yourself up by putting people down, but in [our] society, we tend to do that. The big guys can't be that good; let's find something wrong with them."

We read the histories of Ray Kroc and see that he was confronted with obstacles as he built McDonald's into the franchising giant it is today. We see that Sam Walton experienced the same kind of resistance as he changed the way merchandising was done across our country. As Robert Slater said of the attacks on Wal-Mart, "It was not the media's job to analyze whether the assaults on Wal-Mart were motivated by individuals and groups with hostile intentions toward the company. Its job was to decide whether there was a story worth printing. Finding something wrong was bound to resonate with the media . . . "

To quote Maury Klein once again, "This process of 'Creative Destruction' is the essential fact about capitalism. In virtually every field of endeavor or production, innovation brought with it obsolescence of some kind."

Wal-Mart was upsetting variety store chains that were charging too much for their products. McDonald's was upsetting local restaurants that had poor service and high prices. And the LIFE business, existing as it does at the intersection of four other industries, flies in the face of all conventions. We were quite certain someone wouldn't like it. Perhaps Seth Godin in *The Purple Cow* best explains this whole phenomenon, "If you're remarkable, it's likely that some people won't like you. That's part of the definition of remarkable. Nobody gets unanimous praise, ever. The best the timid can hope for is to be unnoticed. Criticism comes to those who stand out."

> "If you're remarkable, it's likely that some people won't like you. That's part of the definition of remarkable. Nobody gets unanimous praise, ever. The best the timid can hope for is to be unnoticed. Criticism comes to those who stand out."
> -Seth Godin

To succeed in business it takes an ability to run one's own race. We call it Dream, Struggle, Victory. And for some reason, it usually goes in that order. The door to the room of success swings on the hinges of opposition. Anyone in the LIFE business will likely encounter some resistance on the way to victory, but that's just the nature of the battle. Resistance is the seasoning that makes success taste sweet. Nothing great was ever accomplished without struggle, and building a successful business will be no exception. It will, however, be worth it.

> *"The credit belongs to the man in the arena, whose face is marred by dust and sweat and blood; who strives valiantly . . ."*
> -Teddy Roosevelt

As Teddy Roosevelt, the United States' youngest president said, "The credit belongs to the man in the arena, whose face is marred by dust and sweat and blood; who strives valiantly . . . who knows the great enthusiasms, the great devotions; who spends himself in a worthy cause; who at the best knows in the end the triumph of high achievement, and who at the worst, if he fails, at least fails while daring greatly so that his place shall never be with those cold and timid souls who have never known neither victory nor defeat."

The Invisible Economy

Dr. R. Buckminster Fuller, a man considered to be one of the most accurate "futurists" of our times, predicted in the early 1980s that we would soon see the death of the Industrial Age. He said it would be hard for most to see the onset of the Information Age because the changes would be invisible. Robert Kiyosaki calls it the "Invisible Economy." He says these industries are "Information Age businesses because they are invisible businesses. Because it is an invisible business, it is often hard to describe the business's benefits to people who think with Industrial Age minds who still try to see the business with their eyes, rather than their minds." Noel Tichy, in *The Cycle of Leadership*, says, "Intangibles have replaced physical goods as the primary conveyors of value."

The point is that the Industrial Age is over and the Information Age is here. But unfortunately, many are still stuck in Industrial Age thinking. They believe that college degrees are the key to success. They think high paying jobs are the ticket to sexy lifestyles.

They think that "doing pretty good" is good enough, when "great" is available. They think Social Security will be around for them upon retirement, and they think their 401k savings plans are secure investments. When they think of businesses, they think of buildings, employees, inventories and things that can be seen.

The LIFE business allows members to operate from the comforts of their homes, work according to their own schedules, and expand wherever they choose. Product stocking, handling, shipping and delivery all happen in the background and are invisible to the LIFE member. Due in large part to this invisibility, it is hard at first for people to understand. They see with their eyes rather than their minds. Because the LIFE business runs only upon word of mouth, people think it's a "pyramid" or a "sign-up" game or some soap-selling thing their parents did, because back in the Industrial Age, that's how those things operated. The LIFE member has no building, no sign on outside

101

with their name on it to show their in-laws how successful they are, no liability costs, very little inventory, no employees, no infrastructure. It doesn't seem like a business when analyzed according to Industrial Age thinking, but proves to be one of the most progressive, aggressive, explosive business ideas once viewed with Information Age thinking. In his book *Self Made in America*, multi-millionaire entrepreneur John McCormack gives the advice, "Go into businesses that are not considered businesses." Exactly.

It first takes a *dream* to make your aim true, then a *struggle* to make you worthy of the prize, followed by a *victory* that makes it all worthwhile. There is no stopping an idea whose time has come. There is no standing in the way of destiny. In the words of Pharaoh in the epic television classic *The Ten Commandments*, "So it is written, so shall it be done." It's the Information Age now, like it or not, and though businesses themselves are largely invisible, even the skeptics can see the results!

11
BUILDING A CULTURE
THE TEAM DIFFERENCE

In Chapter 7 we discussed our "master strategy" which is appropriately labeled the *Team Approach*. As trite as it might sound, we really do believe that Together Everyone Achieves More. However, there is much more to building a successful business team or community than a master strategy or LIFE changing products. There has to be a culture, and that culture has to be created and, for lack of a better word, cultivated. We believe our culture is one of the key components to building the LIFE business.

The first key step in building the right culture is leaders and the leadership they provide. To quote Bill George, "The leader's job is to provide an empowering environment that enables employees to serve their customers and provides them, the training, education, and support they need." These comments ring true in the LIFE business as well. Environments can take many forms, and every organization eventually ends up with a culture of its own. The difference between good organizations and great ones is how much of their culture they create, what it stands for, and how much they leave to chance.

Tom Peters, Author of the best-seller business book *A Passion for Excellence,* made some observations of Southwest Airlines that we feel apply to the Team culture today. Peters said, "Three things I see: being crazy enough to follow an unorthodox vision, being courageous enough to allow people to have fun and be 'real' people who love and care at work, and being smart enough to recognize that their most valuable assets are their people and the culture they create."

Vision, Mission, Purpose

The Team's way of doing things, or its "culture," is full of things both large and small that make all the difference. It begins with the Vision, Mission, and Purpose that we discussed earlier in this book. From that framework, decision-making becomes easier. Things either align with our Vision, Mission and Purpose or they do not. Lou Holtz, former head football coach of national champion Notre Dame said, "Most people have trouble making decisions. But decisions are easy to make if you know what your purpose is."

"Most people have trouble making decisions. But decisions are easy to make if you know what your purpose is."
-Lou Holtz

With a clear focus on purpose, the Team can help people stay the course. A consistent, straightforward direction provides the first step to an exhilarating business culture because everybody knows where the ship is going and why. They learn where they fit in the big picture. From there, it's important to be clear about what the organization stands for, and what the Team stands for is as important as what it does: helping people "Have Fun, Make Money, and Make a Difference."

Policy Council

Another Team difference and core to its culture is its advisory body we call the Policy Council. While many businesses and companies operate according to a "cult of personality" of some individual high-profile leader, a team of leaders guides the direction of the

Team's training system. It is comprised of the most experienced and successful LIFE members. The Policy Council recommends our strategic direction and insures that we stay true to our Vision, Mission and Purpose. We find that this shared power is not unique to the Team, of course, but is a model followed by many of the most successful companies of our time.

Intel, the world's leader in producing microprocessors, was built and run for twenty-five years by a triumvirate of three leaders; Gordon Moore, Bob Noyce, and Andy Grove. Hewlett-Packard was built over a thirty-year period by a close partnership of David Packard and Bill Hewlett. Bill Gates and Paul Allen, along with Steve Ballmer, have coordinated their complementary talents to build Microsoft into a behemoth. The list continues on and on to include Michael Dell and Kevin Rollins at Dell Computer Corp.; Ray Kroc and Harry Sonneborn at McDonald's; John Whitehead and John Weinberg at Goldman Sachs; Roger Enrico and Steve Reinemund at PepsiCo; and Robert Goizeuta and Don Keough at Coca-Cola.

While the authors helped instigate the foundation of the Team training system, we are by no means the only or most important force. Each of the leaders serving on the Policy Council, based on their performance, is vital. They contribute their perspectives, leadership ability, energy, expertise, and direction on the policies and provisions of the Team. In addition, Rob Hallstrand, COO, has brought his tireless dedication and administrative expertise to an entrepreneurial environment with professionalism and class. His staff, headquartered in Flint, Michigan, is comprised of seasoned industry professionals. Their contribution to the overall organization and execution of the Team's system is world-class. As McDonald's founder Ray Kroc said many times, "No one of us is as good as all of us!"

Recognition and Celebration

It could be said that the Team has a culture that teaches people to play as hard as they work. As a matter of fact, we have an entire program called Power Player, in which top performers are not only recognized for being a top player in their business arena, but are also invited to participate in play as recreation. We have taken white-water-rafting trips with the Power Players, raced go-carts and had costume parties; hosted scavenger hunts and held picnics. We like the axiom, "The team that plays together stays together," and when the Team lets down its hair, it's a fun time. We always want to recognize and reward achievement, but at the same time never take ourselves too seriously.

This attitude is nothing new to the corporate world. David Novak, CEO of YUM! Brands, Inc., the parent company of Pizza Hut, Taco Bell, KFC, Long John Silver's and A&W, understands the power of having fun and recognizing performance. In *The Cycle of Leadership*, Noel Tichy says of David Novak, CEO of Yum! Brands, Inc. which includes Pizza Hut, Taco Bell and KFC and others:

> "Building energy in a workforce that is far-flung and widely diverse-ranging from teenagers to grandparents takes a lot of energy from Novak and his colleagues.
>
> What many would find hokey, Novak finds essential to Yum!'s success. He takes every opportunity to create positive emotional energy through recognition, fun and camaraderie. To outsiders, the rituals and symbols of any institution can look silly. But when they are sincere and linked to the values of the organization, they fulfill a deep human need to be connected and energized.

Novak is an avid believer in laughter and playful celebrations of accomplishment. When he was president of KFC, he made a big deal out of giving the "Floppy (rubber) Chicken" award to outstanding performers. For the star performers at Pizza Hut, his presidential award was a "Big Cheese" like the ones worn by Green Bay Packers fans. Taco Bellers get the "Royal Order of the Pepper". He even chose the company's name and New York Stock Exchange symbol (YUM) to be memorable and fun. And he has a leadership development program that he calls Building the Yum Dynasty.

David Novak's *Teachable Point of View* on emotional energy is that he believes that a "recognition culture" is how to get it. 'While the practice of saying thank you and recognizing people for good work wasn't necessarily new to us,' he says, 'the idea of identifying those things as a way to grow our business was a little different...We're a company full of awards, from stars to smiley faces to boomerangs to magnets to crystal trophies to CHAMPS cards. And that's just a small sampling of the tangible stuff. We're also overflowing with smiles, applause, cheers, thanks, high-fives, handshakes, voicemails, e-mails, thank you notes, banners, kudos and so much more.'

As frivolous as this may sound, Novak is sincere, and his people know it and love it. It generates a lot of emotional energy and he personally coaches managers on how to do the same."

David Novak and Yum! Brands, Inc., is not alone. In his book *The WalMart Decade* Robert Slater describes WalMart's annual shareholder's meeting:

107

"No other company in the world puts on a show for shareholders quite this spectacular. One after another, executives race to the stage, adrenaline pumping, fist waving and smiles on their faces. Roaring with approval, the crowds pour their hearts and souls into an event that has all the trappings of a pep rally or a political convention.

Wal-Mart turns its event into to a wild week-long celebration, replete with canoe rides, concerts, fireworks, seminars, visits to a company distribution center, and, lest anyone forget why they had all come together, tours of the home office in Bentonville...More in keeping with a sporting than a corporate gathering, the visitors wear every possible combination of company buttons and banners and hats. The red hats and banners identify one Wal-Mart division, the green another. The reds and greens applaud and scream unendingly, but save the loudest roars for that golden moment when someone on the stage mentions the name of their division. Then a section of the arena erupts, and you really feel as if someone has just scored the game-winning basket for the home team.

The Wal-Mart audience – 'First Lady' Helen Walton and her four children, executives, rank-and-file employees, the board of directors, shareholders – gather here on this day with one purpose in mind: to rejoice. Every year they travel – some of them thousands of miles – to take part in this corporate festival with the dual purpose of learning more about the place at which they work and to celebrate the achievements of the past year."

Although we don't wear cheese hats (okay, okay some of our teammates in Wisconsin do!!) or hand out rubber chickens (alas, these ideas were already taken), the Team likewise celebrates what is important in properly building a LIFE business, and shines the spotlight on those teams and individuals that are progressing and achieving. Oh yeah, and we have a lot of fun doing it. And if you perform, we'll find you and recognize you. Why? Because, as these great companies have shown, when an organization believes in people and gives them the recognition and appreciation they deserve, it helps them rise to greatness.

Meetings and Mentorship

As in the case of Yum! Brands, Inc., and Wal-Mart, discussed above, one of the Team's most effective tools is its program of national meetings designed to teach, train, inform, inspire and provide focus to business owners. Also, these events become a format to recognize and celebrate achievements as people build their businesses. Association with like-minded people in pursuit of similar goals is directly beneficial, especially when combined with first-hand information flow from people who have the "fruit on the tree" and have experienced success. The meetings provide a continuous, effective backdrop for learning and building the LIFE business. These events and others are combined with mentorship to give the guidance necessary to walk the path through the minefield. In recent years the scope and number of locations for each type of event have expanded rapidly, increasing even further their effectiveness and geographic reach.

Jeff Immelt, the CEO of GE and successor to the legendary Jack Welch said, "We recruit. We train. We educate. We coach. We spend a ton of time developing people. I probably spend 40 percent of my time... selecting, coaching, deciding who gets which jobs. People are a big part."

109

As we listen to the stories of the most successful LIFE members featured on training materials and at events, we see a consistent pattern: participation in the various meetings available to them was one of the key factors in their business success. One of these successful leaders, Policy Council member Tim Marks recently said to us: "I was not very interested in going to my first 'Major Function,' but within the first two hours of that meeting I got the basis for what I needed to reach my financial goals." Belief and understanding are best accomplished by getting the facts from the people who have them. It is at these meetings where people discover the truth of business owners who like to say, "If you knew what we knew, you'd do what we do."

> As we listen to the stories of our most successful members of the Team, we see a consistent pattern: participation in the various meetings available to them as business owners was one of the key factors in their business success.

Competition Breeds Cooperation

The Team hosts several internal competitions that help spur businesses forward. We have found that people will strive for individual achievement, but pull out all the stops to help their team (think Wal-Mart red hats!) win. Individual reward is heightened by contribution to team success. Also, competition keeps us honest and makes LIFE even more interesting. A favorite quote says, "The other runners in a race are only there to keep you honest and ensure that you actually give it your best effort." It's the old adage of iron sharpening iron.

Team Training Materials

As we discussed in Chapter 4, one of the key components to the Team's approach is the use of a franchise-type philosophy in helping people to build their LIFE businesses. Remember, franchising works primarily because all of the franchisees (think LIFE members) are following the same business building system, and one of the key vehicles for accomplishing this duplicate-able pattern is the wide array of training materials made available to LIFE members by the Team.

People can choose not to participate in any form of the system provided by the Team. Our experience has taught us that people's ultimate goals and dreams will be the greatest influencer of their use of any training system. However, we believe strongly in our approach, system, and master strategy to help people build their LIFE businesses. Top leaders all over the continent do, as well!

The Team has built a business support system especially designed to allow LIFE members to become trained, for the most part, during their idle time; such as listening to CDs while commuting to a job, attending a seminar for a few hours once a month, and a few weekends a year in a more intense training and recognition environment. Such simplicity and convenience, as well as the effectiveness of the information itself, have made the Team training system extremely popular for LIFE members across the continent. Some LIFE members also share in the profits from the sale of the Team training materials.

A Winning Comparison

In our opinion, another large contributing factor to the spread of the LIFE business is the way our information marketing business models stacks up against conventional businesses. It is a low risk entry, easily learned, open-to-everyone situation with a virtually unlimited upside. Very few business models can make such claims.

Conventional Merchandising Business	The LIFE Business
Large Inventory	Small Inventory
Employees or long hours for the owner	No Employees
Own or Lease Space	No Building
Usually Require Large Amounts of Funding	No Significant Capital Outlay
Almost Always Involve Business Debt	No Debt
Standard Accounts Receivables	No Accounts Receivables
No Training System	Extensive Training System
Duplication Only if Franchise Affiliated	Systematized Duplication
Limited Incomes	Unlimited Up Side
Complexity Increases with Size	Complexity Does Not Increase
Usually No Mentorship Available	Mentorship Provided
On Your Own	Win-Win Success Partnership
Confined to the Location	Geographically Unrestricted
Difficult to Expand	Easily Expandable
Must Be Open to Public's Hours	Part Time According to One's Schedule
May Require Full Time Commitment	Can Run While Still Have Job
Product Line Limited by Space Expansion	Unlimited Potential for Product
Dependent on Economy	Economy Proof

While this comparison could be expanded indefinitely, we think it is clear why so many people like the "turn-key" features and low risk involved.

Results

"Don't tell me about the labor pains, show me the baby," said the humorist Jeanne Robertson. Nothing speaks like results. No amount of packaging, hype or self-congratulations can disguise a lack of results, and conversely, no amount of humility or smear from outsiders can diminish it. There is no success quite like success. The scoreboard doesn't lie, and it cannot be ignored. All the talk in this chapter about culture is great, but if it doesn't deliver then it's not worth discussing.

The LIFE business has experienced wonderful growth, and we will not take credit that it's because of our brilliance (but feel free to argue with us about it). We know we have been blessed. But we could not complete this section without confirming, just a little, that the Team system works in helping LIFE members and customers grow.

In our experience, one of the most accurate measures of business health is the number of LIFE members attending Team training events. This is because the product volumes and merchandising levels have an averaging effect across large numbers of participants. There are higher and lower performers, but we see consistent correlations between the vital business numbers and the attendance at events. The Team has developed some of the largest crowds and best-attended training seminars to be found anywhere in the world.

> *The Team has developed some of the largest crowds and best-attended training seminars to be found anywhere in the world.*

* * *

There are many nuances to the LIFE business and Team training system that account for their growth. The few chosen for discussion in this chapter were selected to capture a little of the essence of the LIFE business, the Team training system, and their culture. They all go together to form what some have called a "leadership factory" or "success machine" to propel people toward their life's dreams. Others have called it a vehicle that moves forward on a road of business opportunity. But just like any vehicle, for it to be useful, it needs a driver.

12

A Fork in the Road

We will assume that if you've read this far, you have some level of interest in a LIFE membership. We congratulate you on hanging in there with us through these pages because success begins with information from the correct source.

When people begin in business they sometimes receive opinions from many uninformed sources. There are those who think they know all about what their friends are getting involved with, some who give negative inputs, and some who try to create doubts. We eventually learned to help people sort through these inconsistencies by putting them into three categories:

1. Almost without exception people are not living the lifestyle people want and therefore have no credibility when it comes to giving financial advice.
2. They have no vested interest in seeing people succeed, anyway.
3. They have nothing better to offer.

The beauty of the LIFE business lies in the answers to these three points.

First, anybody who chooses to become a LIFE member participating in the Team training system will have access to teaching and mentoring from people

115

who are living lifestyles that represent solid financial success in the same endeavor.

Second, the very nature of this industry, when properly conducted, is win-win; its very structure is a system of reward tied directly to one's ability to help others succeed.

Third, we believe there is nothing better people can find to do with their energies.

It was the "What If?" questions that got us. What if it would work? What if we could get out of debt and leave our jobs at an early age? What if we could actually accumulate some savings? What if we could build our dream home? What if we could relieve the financial strains of life? What if we could accomplish something of significance? What if we could help other people? What if we could grow personally and learn to help others do the same? What if we could travel? What if we could leave a legacy?

We knew fulfilling such dreams wouldn't be easy, but we decided we didn't want cheap success; we were willing to earn it.

We knew fulfilling such dreams wouldn't be easy, but we decided we didn't want cheap success; we were willing to earn it. We knew someday we would be sitting around a campfire with our grandchildren. We wanted to have a story to tell. We wanted to be able to say our life counted; we had some fun, helped some people, fought our battles, made some money, lived some adventures, and made a difference. We wanted to tell them that when the LIFE business was born, and when it grew to make a positive impact in the lives of a million people, we were there! There was a Leadership Revolution, and we were right smack in the middle of it!

We wanted to tell them that when the LIFE business was born, and when it grew to make a positive impact in the lives of a million people, we were there! There was a Leadership Revolution, and we were right smack in the middle of it!

We know that LIFE is not for everyone:
Some people are ambitious, and some are not.
Some people are looking, and some are not.
Some people are teachable, and some are not.
And regretfully, some people are honest, and
  some are not.
It comes down to a personal choice.

There is a simple exercise that is flexible and can be applied to any real decision one makes in life. It's called "You Decide," and it works like this:

1. Make a list down the left side of a piece of paper itemizing any ways you can think of to generate more income or assets in life.

2. Make a list across the top of the paper listing the following relevant questions to ask before venturing into any income endeavor:

    a. What's the best that can happen if it works?
    b. What's the worst that can happen if it doesn't work?
    c. What does victory look like?
    d. Can I afford to begin it?
    e. Is it something that can be learned?
    f. When will it pay off?
    g. What do I have to give up?
    h. What's the long term potential?
    i. Does it require talents, and if so, do I have them?
    j. Is it effected by the economy?
    k. Is it legal, moral, and honest?
    l. Can I leave it to my children?
    m. Is this based solely on my own efforts?
    n. Is it restricted geographically?
    o. Can I choose who to work with?
    p. Does it make a difference?

q. Are those who succeed happy?
r. Would you do it again?
s. Who determines your success?
t. Can I do it?

3. Put an "X" in each spot that corresponds to a combination that seems positive.
4. Determine which option generated the most "X"s to determine the best choice.

Here is an example:
With few exceptions, this analysis results in a pretty clear picture that the LIFE business is a worthwhile endeavor for many, many people.

	BEST THAT CAN HAPPEN	WORST THAT CAN HAPPEN	WHAT DOES VICTORY LOOK LIKE	HOW DO I LEARN IT	WHEN WILL IT PAY OFF	WHAT DO I HAVE TO GIVE UP	WHAT'S THE LONG TERM POTENTIAL	CAN I AFFORD IT	WHAT TALENTS/SKILLS ARE NEED	IS IT EFFECTED BY ECONOMY	IS THIS BASED SOLELY ON MY OWN EFFORTS	IS IT RESTRICTED GEOGRAPHICALLY	IS IT REPUTABLE	CAN I CHOOSE WHO TO WORK WITH	CAN I LEAVE IT TO MY CHILDREN	DOES IT MAKE A DIFFERENCE	ARE THOSE WHO SUCCEED HAPPY	WOULD YOU DO IT AGAIN	WHO DETERMINES YOUR SUCCESS	CAN I DO IT
REAL ESTATE		X					X			X										
MORE COLLEGE	X					X														X
OVERTIME									X											
FOOD INDUSTRY			X														X	X		
SERVICE INDUSTRY	X							X												
PROFESSIONAL		X					X													
MANUFACTURING		X				X														
SECOND JOB				X																
SPOUSE TO WORK									X											
INVESTOR	X			X																
BUY BUSINESS					X			X									X			
ARTIST					X															
OTHER																				
LIFE WITH THE TEAM	X	X	X	X	X	X	X	X	X	X	X	X	X	X	X	X	X	X	X	X

There are a lot of "good" things people can do. There are a few "great" things to do. There can be only one "best" thing to do. Each person has his/her own specific destiny and path to follow in life. As for us, when we analyze our personal matrices, we want to sign up for LIFE all over again!

James Henri Poincare said, "To doubt everything or to believe everything are two equally convenient solutions; both dispense with the necessity of reflection." With that in mind, we hope this little technique has been helpful to you for reflecting on the choices you face in your financial life. We further hope these pages have opened your eyes to the possibility of a bright financial future.

It is said that Sam Walton, toward the end of his life, expressed the regret that he wouldn't be around to see Wal-Mart become the biggest company in the world. He supposedly would lie awake at night thinking about the potential left in his incredible business. He was excited about the countless little towns across America with at least five thousand people in them, each a prime target for a new Wal-Mart store.

If Sam Walton got that excited about how many towns of five thousand people were still untapped, then those of us involved with the LIFE business are beside ourselves with excitement over how many "individuals" are out there! How many more people across the country and around the world are sick and tired of being sick and tired? How many are looking for a better way, or for some, a way out? How many others are there like the ones we've found so far? How many are like Henry David Thoreau and are "leading lives of quiet desperation?" How many are ambitious, looking, teachable, and honest? Now you can see why we said at the front of this book that we've only just begun. There is so much more to do!

In the previous chapter we ended by saying this is a great growth vehicle, but it needs a driver. If you choose to become one, we recommend you fasten your seat belt! It's an incredible journey!

"There is a tide in the affairs of men,
Which, taken at the flood, leads on to fortune...
On such a full sea are we now afloat,
And we must take the current when it comes,
Or lose our ventures."
- William Shakespeare, *Julius Caesar*

13
A Vision for the Future
Going Main Stream

We've covered a lot in this book. If we said no more, hopefully we've given you enough to understand the magnitude and potential of the LIFE business and how your involvement in it could be very beneficial. However, we can't let you go without casting a little bit of a vision for where we think the industry can, should, and must go! This won't all happen tomorrow, but it is ripe for the picking, and somebody will do it!

A Million People

The Team has long held the vision that the Team's training system would someday seat over 1 million people at its training events around the world at one time! This number also represents an accomplishment never before achieved by any training system in this industry.

Three Train Wrecks

This book has attempted to explain our exciting business environment and the trends that all come together to make the LIFE business such a great place to invest time and effort. However, there may be an even easier way to explain what we do. We call the concept the "Three Train Wrecks." What we have observed is that most people in life are headed for at least one of three possible train wrecks in their lives.

The first category in which people may be headed for disaster is in their health. Unfortunately, for many people there will come a day when they are sitting in a doctor's office somewhere on that squishy, padded examination table with the "butcher" paper rolled out across it. And they will be receiving some bad news. A lifetime of neglect, poor habits, bad diet, or whatever will have finally caught up with them. If you or someone you love has ever experienced such a moment you can attest to the shock and fear that accompanies it. Further, there is only so much that can be done once our bodies have been damaged. They can medicate, or maybe operate, but in the vast amount of cases the person will never be quite the same. It is too late.

The second category in which people may be headed for a train wreck is in their finances. Some of you reading this may have already experienced one or two in your life! The number of personal bankruptcies filed each year is staggering. Credit card debt and "upside down" mortgages are too common. Savings are nonexistent for way too many people. And to top it all off the economy is in pretty flimsy shape and even the United States government has a problem with fiscal responsibility! As Ronald Reagan famously said, "A recession is when your neighbor loses his job, a depression is when you lose yours!" Many people have less financial security than they would like, and they are hanging on the thread of whether or not someone will continue to employ them. Good money management and what has been called "financial intelligence" are rare. And even for people who are pretty adept at saving and managing their money, disaster still strikes from time to time, eliminating "rainy day" savings when a flood comes! What most people need is an opportunity where they can legitimately prosper financially for their efforts. They need true free enterprise.

The third category in which many people will or are already experiencing a train wreck is in their wisdom. Wisdom can be defined as applying the right principle at the right time. Wisdom is learning from experience, and, of course, the best experience is somebody else's. This saves time and heartache. Wisdom is the only way off the time and/or relationship train wreck. We are constantly amazed at the number of people who aren't on speaking terms with their own mother, father, brother, sister, aunt or uncle. There is nothing so painful and debilitating as a broken heart, hurt feelings, and relational conflict. There are some people we've observed who seem to be in a state of combat with most people in their lives. This is an unhappy and unnecessary condition. Also, wisdom means understanding the power of leverage in your financial life. We have spoken at length about this concept in this book. Leveraging a system to do the work for you is one of the wisest ways to go about putting effort into something.

The LIFE business specializes in delivering solutions to people who are either experiencing, or will experience, train wrecks in these critical areas of life. By providing world-class information and training, mentorship and example, along with a productive community-based environment, people can be given the answers, guidance, and encouragement they need to make lasting changes for the better.

Further, by providing people with a world-class financial opportunity we can help them produce a secondary or even primary income source to alleviate financial stress and prevent economic ruin. And finally, by delivering a training system that develops wisdom in the arts of personal relationships, community development, and building teams, people will not only learn "wealth thinking" regarding their finances and the building of a business, but they will grow in their emotional and relational intelligence. This leads to stronger, healthier relationships and the peace and happiness that result from deep, lasting bonds with people.

We know that no matter whom we talk to out there in the world, they are likely headed for at least one of these possible trains wrecks. What makes us so passionate about spreading this great concept of the LIFE business around the world is that we have seen first hand the power it has in changing and improving lives. Watch someone dig themselves out of financial bondage and you will be filled with joy. Observe someone getting fit and experiencing the best feeling of wellbeing and overall health they've had in decades and realize that you are doing a great thing. And experience the first-hand benefit of better relationships and the power of a community of people aligned in common purpose, and you will realize that in such harmony is how we were built to exist.

Does all this sound just a little too idealistic? We hope so, because we never want to allow life's challenges and struggles to make us jaded. We will firmly hold to the belief that helping others prosper and grow and lead healthier lives is a worthy cause for which we will continue to devote our time, energy, and love. We love what we do with the LIFE business because we understand just how bad these three train wrecks can be in a person's life and we are committed to making a difference by helping people avoid them!

A Tale of Three Industries

Although each of their origins can be traced back to the early 1900s, there are three industries that were officially born sometime in the post-World War II economic boom.

One of these industries was what we'll call mass-merchandise discounting, and we've already talked a lot about it in this book. Mass-merchandise dis-

124

counting, which might more readily today be called "Big Box Stores," was pioneered by Sam Walton of Wal-Mart fame. Not only did Walton's concept become "main stream," but also at hundreds of billions of dollars in revenue, it could fairly be considered to be the stream! Add to that the other competing companies and those built upon the same model, such as Target, Costco, Best Buy, Circuit City, and a host of others, and one gets the idea of the enormity of this segment of our world economy.

The second of these three industries has also received a lot of coverage in the pages of this book. Ray Kroc, the founder of McDonald's, finally took franchising out of the Dark Ages. His efforts were so successful and so successfully duplicated that any world traveler can attest to the ability to step off a plane in nearly any part of the world and find a franchise food establishment somewhere near by. It's gotten to the point where we almost expect it!

The third industry, which you may have guessed by now, is what we have called networking earlier in the book. Although it was birthed at roughly the same time as the other two industries, and it even grew at relatively comparable rates in its early history, something happened that prevented its rise to "mainstream." The reasons for this are not the topic of this book, however, the fact remains: networking was once on track to be just as large and just as dominant as big box stores and franchising! We believe that there is no reason it shouldn't still become mainstream! All that would be required is a product with massive customer enthusiasm, a compensation plan that actually allows people to prosper through their hard work, and a corporation that understands treating its members with the utmost respect is the key to continuing growth and strength in the marketplace.

All of these things come to fruition with the LIFE business, which, interestingly, isn't merely networking at all. In order to take the concept mainstream, our concept actually takes the intersection of four exciting trends and puts them all together, taking the good from each and leaving the bad, as we explained in Chapter 2. The way to go mainstream with the concepts of personal business ownership, word-of-mouth information marketing, and community building, is to create a whole new industry. That's exactly what the LIFE business is currently doing.

It's the power of an idea whose time has come—actually, an idea whose time is thirty years behind where it should have been already! There is effectively a thirty-year vacuum that must be filled. There is a lot of revenue, a lot of success, and a lot of growth that must happen quickly to fill that void. In effect, the new industry created by the LIFE business is going mainstream!

Why shouldn't LIFE be as common as a Visa card, (only more valuable in people's lives)? Why shouldn't millions of people be profiting from the incredible LIFE compensation plan? There is nothing stopping these visions from becoming reality. All that is needed is leaders and participants to help make it so. And that, dear reader, is where the real opportunity lies.

Welcome to the LIFE you've always wanted!

As Victor Hugo said, "An invasion of armies can be resisted, but not an idea whose time has come." Welcome aboard.

FURTHER RESEARCH

For more information about the LIFE business, LIFE membership, or becoming a LIFE subscriber, please visit www.life-leadership-home.com (US) or www.life-leadership-home.ca (Canada).

For additional product and member information, visit _____, the personal home page of the person who handed you this book.

A copy of the LIFE business Income Disclosure Statement (IDS) for the US is available at www.life-leadership-home.com, and the Statement of Typical Participant Earnings (STPE) for Canada is included in the LIFE Compensation Plan and is available at www.life-leadership-home.ca.

SOURCES

Collins, Jim. Good to Great: *Why Some Companies Make the Leap . . .* and Others Don't. New York: Harper Business, 2001.

De Blasi, Marlena. *That Summer in Sicily: A Love Story.* New York: Ballantine Books, The Random House Publishing Group, 2008.

DeGeorge, Gail. *The Making of a Blockbuster.* John Wiley & Sons, Inc., 1996.

Dell, Michael. *Direct from Dell.* New York: Harper Business, 1999.

Dell, Michael. *Building a Competitive Advantage in an Internet Economy.* Speech delivered at the Detroit Economic Club Luncheon, Detroit, MI. November 1, 1999.

Eldredge, John. *Wild at Heart,* Discovering the Secret of a Man's Soul. Nashville: Thomas Nelson, Inc., 2001

Freiberg, Kevin and Jackie. *Nuts! Southwest Airline's Crazy Recipe for Business and Personal Success.* New York: Broadway Books, 1996.

Getty, Paul, J. *How To Be Rich.* Chicago: Playboy Press, 1961.

George, Bill. *Authentic Leadership: Rediscovering the Secrets to Creating Lasting Value.* San Francisco: Jossey-Bass, 2003.

Gerber, Michael E. *The E Myth Revisited.* New York: Harper Collins, 1995.

Godin, Seth. *The Purple Cow: Transform Your Business By Being Remarkable.* New York: Penguin, 2002.

Griffith, Joe. *Speaker's Library of Business Stories, Anecdotes and Humor.* New Jersey: Prentice Hall, 1990.

Hales, Dianne. *La Bella Lingua: My Love Affair With Italian, The World's Most Enchanting Language.* New York: Broadway Books, Crown Publishing Group, 2009.

Hedges, Burke. *Dream-Biz.com: Design Your Future and Live Your Dreams in the e-Economy!* Tampa: INTI Publishing, 1999.

Hedges, Burke. *The Parable of the Pipeline: How Anyone Can Build A Pipeline of Ongoing Residual Income In The New Economy.* Tampa: INTI Publishing, 2001.

Holy Bible: *New King James Version.* New York: Thomas Nelson Publishers Inc., 1979.

Kiyosaki, Robert T. *Rich Dad's Prophecy.* New York: Warner Books, 2002.

Kiyosaki, Robert T. *The CASHFLOW Quadrant®: Rich Dad's Guide to Financial Freedom.* New York: Warner Books, 1998.

Klein, Maury. *The Change Makers: From Carnegie to Gates, How the GREAT ENTREPRENUERS Transformed Ideas into Industries.* New York: Times Books, 2003.

Love, John F. *McDonald's: Behind the Arches.* New York: Bantam Books, 1986.

Luecke, Richard. *Scuttle Your Ships Before Advancing, And Other Lessons from History on Leadership and Change for Today's Managers.* New York: Oxford University Press, 1994.

Maxwell, John C. *The 21 Irrefutable Laws of Leadership: Follow Them and People Will Follow You.* Nashville: Nelson, 1998.

Maxwell, John C. *Thinking For a Change.* New York: Warner Business Books, 2003.

McCormack, John. *Self-Made In America.* New York: Addison Wesley, 1990.

O' Boyle, Jane. *Wrong! The Biggest Mistakes and Miscalculations Ever Made by People Who Should Have Known Better.* New York: Penguin Group, 1999.

Perot, Ross. *My Life & The Principles For Success.* Arlington: Summit, 1996.

Pilzer, Paul Zane. *The Next Millionaires.* Texas: Momentom Media, 2006.

Slater, Robert. *The Wal-Mart Decade, How a New Generation of Leaders Turned Sam Walton's Legacy into the World's #1 Company.* New York: Penguin Group, 2003.

Stanley, Andy. *Visioneering, God's blueprint for developing and maintaining personal vision.* Sisters: Multnomah Publishers, Inc., 1999.

Tichy, Noel M. *The Cycle of Leadership*. New York: HarperCollins, 2002.

Tracy, Brian. *Eat That Frog*. San Francisco: Berreti-Koehler Publishers, Inc., 2002.

Walton, Sam and Huey, John. Sam Walton: *Made in America, My Story*. New York: Doubleday, 1992.